AN ECHO IN ANOTHER'S MIND

First published July 1994
by Quest Books (NI)
2 Slievenabrock Avenue, Newcastle, Co. Down, N. Ireland. BT33 0HZ.

Typeset by December Publications, Belfast
Printed in Northern Ireland by
The University Press (Belfast) Limited

A catalogue record of this book is available from
The British Library

ISBN 1-872027-06-7

Front cover by Carousel Design

Maps by Carousel Design and the author

Photographs by the author

AN ECHO IN ANOTHER'S MIND

BERT SLADER

*Echoes of the people and the mountains
of Ireland and Abroad*

QUEST BOOKS (NI)

The Valley of Echoes

CONTENTS

ACKNOWLEDGEMENTS

My thanks are due to everyone who features in these tales. Their friendship and help were freely given. Their fortitude sustained me. Their humour, resourcefulness and forbearance were vital elements of every episode recounted.

Yvonne and Deirdre who appear in Chapter 7 lent me their memories, a diary of the walk and their photographs.

My thanks are due too, to my friends and family for their help and patience.

These stories are echoes of some of the most memorable times in my life and I will always be grateful to those who shared them with me.

AN ECHO IN ANOTHER'S MIND is dedicated to:

all those who made the echoes, and listened too.

To the silent wilderness
Where the soul need not repress
Its music lest it should not find
An echo in another's mind.

Percy Bysshe Shelley
after whom a Mourne crag is named

THE SLEDGE HAMMER THAT BUILT THE MOURNE WALL

World War 2 had just ended the previous year and we were sixteen when we went to the Mourne Mountains for the first time. No one organised the trip for us, or took us there, or described the mountains, or warned us of the dangers, or told us what to wear, or showed us how to use a map and compass.

John and I went by train. At the time there were two railway lines from Belfast to Newcastle, the Belfast and County Down and the Great Northern via Banbridge. We chose the GNR, although it was a much longer journey, and arrived in the village of Ballyward one dark afternoon in January.

It was in the very depths of the hardest winter for years, the countryside was covered with snow, with ice on the ponds and frozen snow on the hedges. The shortest way to the youth hostel was a complicated route through twisting lanes and side roads. On the map the distance measured eight miles. It felt much longer.

We found Slievenaman Youth Hostel in a beautiful valley under the mountains. No one else was booked in. The warden lived in the farm house nearby and having the place to ourselves, it felt as if we had booked the hostel as our private residence for the night.

We stoked up the fire with logs and coal and slept in front of the hearth. It gave us warmth and comfort for hours but died before dawn and the cold had us up and making breakfast far earlier than intended.

That day we crossed the mountains from north to south by a road we never saw. The tarmac was deep in snow, without car tracks or human footprints. The surrounding peaks were frosted domes except one which had two sharp, ice-streaked, rocky summits. The frozen crust creaked underfoot. It was a vast Arctic landscape, empty of people, as brightly glistening as I would find years later inside the Arctic Circle itself.

Droppings and hoof marks showed the way the sheep had crossed. A white hare ran the white slope above, effortlessly, without apprehension. Telephone poles marked the way, but even with their presence the winter had taken us back through the centuries. It was not imagination. We were

1

on the ancient route across the mountains from the sheep fair town of Hilltown to Kilkeel, capital of the Mourne Country.

We stayed in the hostel at the Silent Valley and this time there was company. After a few days two recently de-mobbed soldiers with ice axes and a climbing rope arrived. They were obviously missing the excitement of war and told us that they had been commandos. The previous evening they had 'borrowed' a boat to cross Carlingford Lough when they had found the ferry was not operating and had slept in a field that night.

There was also in residence a young man with his girl friend, both a few years older than we were. Foolishly the young man allowed the ex-soldiers to persuade him to join them on an ascent of Slieve Binnian in the ice and snow. When they arrived back much later than expected the young man looked exhausted and miserable, and in the early stages of exposure. He had probably done well. Although unimpressed by his performance, they had kindly lent him a pair of thin water-proof over-trousers to put on over his shorts when he complained of the cold.

Privately John and I congratulated each other on our astute judgement in refusing the invitation to join the party that morning. The ex-commandos had been very persuasive, almost making it a test of our manhood. But we had no thoughts of joining them. Our own plans had been made and we needed to be fit and fresh for the next day.

In the morning we returned to Slievenaman through the heart of the mountains, clutching the map and compass like a sailor's life-line. Every few steps we checked the map, looking for a mountain or a river we could identify in this wonderful snow laden landscape.

Our route lay almost directly north, past Lough Shannagh, the largest lake in the Mournes. But the lough was hidden amongst the peaks. Here we were in the heart of the mountains, well away from roads. This snow and ice clad terrain was how I imagined the Alps would be. The Mournes are neither high nor extensive but they are a compact group of hills, with a great number of peaks close together, rising steeply from valleys virtually at sea-level.

We glanced behind us and saw a stretch of water between two mountains. Was it Lough Shannagh? Could we be travelling in exactly the wrong direction? I checked the compass and it seemed as if we were right. Could the compass be wrong? Could it be affected by iron ore in the ground? Perhaps it was broken.

We had been carrying the map folded carefully to show our route. Now we opened it out and solved the problem. The stretch of water behind us was a tiny glimpse of the sea. It was Carlingford Lough to our rear, not Lough Shannagh.

We laughed with relief. It takes only the smallest uncertainty to erode the confidence of the inexperienced navigator and of such uncertainties tragedies are often born. But solve the little problems and the boost to the confidence may last the mountaineer a lifetime.

We learned by doing. At one stage we climbed a peak to get our bearings. It was smaller than the main mountains but its lower slopes were steep and it had a wonderful rocky knob as a summit. It was un-named on our map so we christened it Sladridges. A few years later I found it had a name, Doan, and it was a great relief to drop the embarrassing pretension of associating our names with such a magnificent peak.

This was a time of austerity and strict food rationing. Although the war had ended the previous year, the ration of some foodstuffs was now smaller than it had been during the hostilities. However, when we descended from the hills to the first farm there was food a-plenty.

For a few shillings we bought a dozen eggs, twenty potatoes, a cake of wheaten bread, two pints of milk and a cabbage. Of the stores we had brought from home there was a tin of corned beef left and a few rashers of bacon. With what we had bought it might just be enough to do us for dinner and breakfast.

We returned the next year and Harry came with us. We wore shorts for walking as before and, although there was snow only on the summits, it seemed much colder than before. John and I joked about paddling in Lough Shannagh to ease the tired feet. But when we reached the lough, we were amazed to see Harry sit on a stone and take off his boots and socks. He threw a few rocks to break the ice at the edge of the lake and sauntered in to the water up to his knees.

"What's keeping you?" He made it sound as if we were committed to joining him. "After all the stories about last year I thought you hard men would be peeling off for a swim."

John sauntered into the lake with his boots on and with a grand air which must have served him well in later life as an eminent physician. I sat down to take off my boots as slowly as possible. I reckoned that the longer it took, the shorter I would have to stay in the lake. I was wrong. They insisted I do the same stint as themselves. It was only their jeers that kept me in that freezing lake until honour was satisfied.

There is usually a reward for such mortification of the flesh, although the wait is sometimes long and return may be retribution rather than recompense. Ours came as soon as we had dried our feet and replaced our socks and boots. In John's case that meant shaking the water from his boots and using a dry pair of socks. The feet felt renewed, revitalised, ready for any challenge we could offer them.

It was the beginning of a life-long affection for the Mournes for me. Alone or with a few friends I wandered the mountains, camping in hidden places, never with anyone who knew the peaks or was an experienced mountaineer. It was learning by doing, by being there.

We had no thought of bagging peaks. An ascent was for the view or, as John and I had done on that first adventure, to find the way. There was no inclination to do long walks at top speed, no great sense of achievement at so many miles covered or so many feet climbed, no feeling of conquering the mountains. It was enough to be there.

From the beginning it was the travelling and living amongst the mountains that meant more to me than the climbing peaks. It was the journey through the hills that brought me there.

A year later I did decide to climb a peak. The mountain with the two rocky pinnacles at its summit, which John and I had seen on our first day in these hills, was the most dramatic peak of all. It was not as high as Slieve Donard. But whereas Donard was a great lump of a mountain, Slieve Bernagh rose sharply to its summit tors like the shapely spires of the Alps.

I walked from Newcastle on a fine summer's day, travelling light. The Glen River path led to the saddle between Slieve Donard and Slieve Commedagh and I followed the Brandy Pad across the hills to the Hare's Gap at the foot of Bernagh.

By tradition the smugglers used the Brandy Pad when taking their contraband from the rocky shore south of Newcastle to the pubs and shops of Hilltown on the other side of the mountains.

It was easy to believe the story. The Pad looked as if it had been travelled by man and pack animal for centuries. It was not a single path but an interwoven tracery of tracks which separated to find the best line, criss-crossed, joined at a point where there was only one good way across a gully.

No wonder there were stories of people being lost in the mist when they thought it would be easy to follow the Pad through the hills. In places one of the many tracks would leave the general line and angle down the slope away from the route to join another path in the valley below. In the mist a walker without map and compass, and of course, the ability to use them, could be misled and find himself coming out of the hills nearer Annalong than Newcastle.

I climbed the steep grassy slopes of Slieve Bernagh and scrambled over the rocky tors at the summit. It felt as if I was truly in the midst of the Mournes. Since I had left the forest at Newcastle I had met no one and here it was easy to believe that I had the hills completely to myself.

The map allowed me to pick out each mountain and lake and try to memorise the name. Although Doan, the one John and I had climbed, was one of the smallest, it was a fine peak and I was pleased that it had been my first ascent rather than one of the better known Slieves. To the west the Mournes were much more spread out than in the east. Each mountain had its own distinctive shape, only Slieve Donard and Slieve Commedagh were similar in form.

Running away from me in two directions was the Mourne Wall. It reached across the highest peaks, encircling the inner area of the Eastern Mournes. It was head height and built of granite blocks, following the watershed ridges and summits. Years later I saw The Great Wall of China at its eastern end where it enters the sea and heard the Chinese call it The Dragon. They would say,

"The Dragon sleeps in the mountains but his head is in the Yellow Sea."

Had St. Patrick not banished all snakes from Ireland, we could have called The Mourne Wall, The Snake, as it lay curled in a great circle, sleeping on the backs of the peaks.

I left the top of Bernagh, loping down the slope at a gentle run. Still feeling energetic, I ran back along the Brandy Pad.

A cold air swirled around me from behind and I turned to see the mist streaming over the pass called the Hare's Gap, borne on a fresh breeze from the west. It closed around me like a grey cloud. In seconds the bright summer day and the great views were gone and I was enveloped in a dense fog. For the first time I was aware of the silence. Losing vision was making me aware of the lack of sound.

All I could see of the Brandy Pad was the next few feet of one little track. I smiled to myself, remembering the slightly smug feeling of 'it couldn't happen to me' when I had heard of others getting lost here, on the Brandy Pad, of all places.

With the map in one hand and the compass in the other I headed south-west, walking quickly, making sure not to lose height. Then my thigh muscles began to cramp in short agonising spasms. The reason seemed obvious. I was not accustomed to running in the hills and the legs were now complaining. Coping with either the mist or the cramp would have been relatively easy but the two together brought a surge of uncertainty, of apprehension.

I knew that I would have to leave the Brandy Pad at a particular point and turn north to cross the pass called the Saddle between Donard and Commedagh. But how would I know when to change direction? All I could see were nearby clumps of heather and rocks and two or three yards of the path in front of me.

Then I had an idea which might solve both problems at once.

Before I reached the point where I should leave the Brandy Pad for the Saddle, I would pass the rocky pinnacles called the Castles of Commedagh. Although I would not be able to see the Castles for the mist, they were split by steep gullies. The Brandy Pad crossed these gullies at points which I remembered. Each required care because of crumbling rock and unstable gravel.

I decided that if I climbed one of these gullies I would reach the Mourne Wall on the Commedagh side of the Saddle and the challenge and excitement of the ascent would help the legs.

The gully I chose had a trickle of water falling down it from ledge to ledge. It was steep and loose. The rocks crumbled to the touch. The gravel spilled away from beneath my feet. I paused at what I decided was 'the point of no return'.

The mist swirled up from below and parted to show narrow pinnacles and walls of banded rock. There was a tiny glimpse of blue sky, as if to tell me that beyond the cloak of vapour that fine summer's day was still there.

The Castles of Commedagh was no fanciful name. These mist wreathed rocks were the turrets and buttresses of the Commedagh's own redoubt. The cramps had disappeared, eased by the body's response to the challenge. I stood on my own, on the tiny broken ledge and savoured the moment. Here was the drama of nature, absent on easy going on a good day, rare indeed in the company of others; but an experience of some significance for those who can feel it.

The top of the gully was steeper and more difficult than I would have wished but the route revealed itself as I climbed. The Mourne Wall was where it should have been, as was the Saddle and I descended to the Glen River and into the sunshine again.

Below me was the curve of Dundrum Bay and I thought I would have a swim off the beach at Newcastle when I arrived. Was ever a town so well placed for the mountains and the sea.?

For a time I avoided Slieve Donard. It was the highest peak at 2,796 feet, the best known, the most climbed mountain in the Mournes. Perhaps it was its popularity which kept me away. It was the peak's history and the insistence of a friend that brought me to it.

Almost as soon as I discovered the mountains I came upon Professor Estyn Evans's book, *'Mourne Country'* and *'The Ancient and Present State of the County Down'* written in the early part of the 18th century by Walter Harris.

These two books published 200 years apart opened the history of the Mournes to me in a way which added a new fascination to each journey in the mountains. Through their pages I could travel back to the past as I walked the hills in the present. From Harris I learned that Slieve Donard was named after St. Domangard, a disciple of St. Patrick who built a cell from stones at the top of the mountain. He lived there as a hermit for many years and after his death local people made an annual pilgrimage to his cell at the summit.

Evans believed the two huge cairns on the summit to be of prehistoric origin. Many years later I was to discover that other authorities considered the pilgrimage to date back to pagan times. It was then part of the great festival of Lughnasa, of which Slieve Donard was one of the foremost sites in all of Ireland.

From Evans I found that a group of Sappers from the Royal Engineers had camped on the summit for nine months at the beginning of the 19th century, during the first map making of Ireland by field survey.

Slieve Donard was becoming an intriguing peak but its popularity still kept me away. It was my friend Arthur who persuaded me to climb Donard. He was familiar with the countryside of the Mournes but new to its peaks. We climbed Donard almost directly from Newcastle on a bitterly cold day in winter. Half way up we stepped on to frozen snow and into a fierce wind from the west.

The two great summit cairns were plastered with snow and the

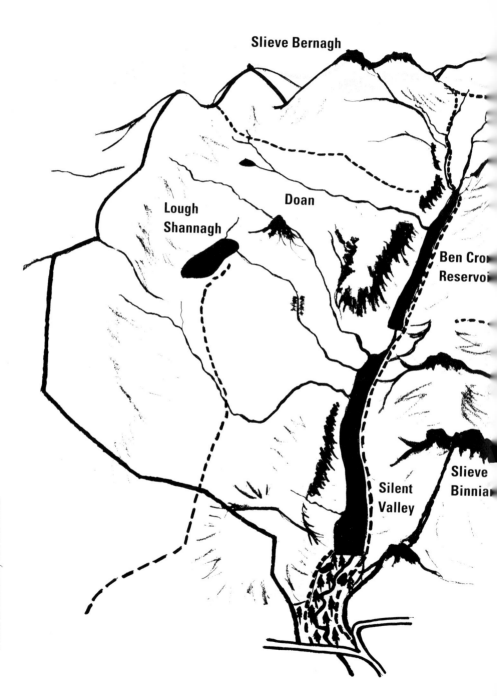

Slieve Bernagh

Doan

Lough Shannagh

Ben Cro[n] Reservoi[r]

Silent Valley

Slieve Binnia[n]

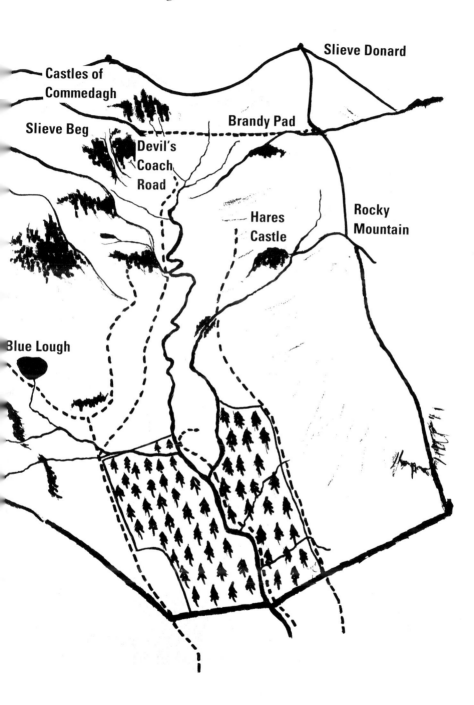

Slieve Donard

Castles of
Commedagh

Brandy Pad

Slieve Beg

Devil's
Coach
Road

Hares
Castle

Rocky
Mountain

Blue Lough

spindrift whipped between them on the wind. We saw the hole that must have been the Sappers' well and the tower at the summit which marks the highest point on the Mourne Wall.

It was easy to appreciate the effect of wind and altitude on the degree of cold we were feeling. There is a temperature drop of 3° Fahrenheit for every 1,000 feet ascended above sea-level. The so-called 'wind-chill factor' means that each mile per hour of wind creates a further effective drop of 1°F. That day the temperature in Newcastle when we left had been 34° Farenheit (2° Celsius). We had climbed nearly 3,000 feet and the wind was at least 20 m.p.h. so the effective temperature must have been 5°F (-14°C). In other words almost 30° Farenheit or 14° Celsius below freezing.

I found a sheltered spot for lunch on the east side. As we sat down to eat out of the wind, the clouds parted and the sun warmed us. Arthur had brought two bottles of beer but the beer was frozen and we had to wait until we were almost down to celebrate the walk.

Forty years later I came upon a note I had made a few weeks before our climb and after a visit to the Reference Library in Belfast. I had been studying Harris's book at the time and the note indicated that the pilgrimage to the summit of Slieve Donard in Christian times took place on the 25 July, St. James's Day. Harris indicated that the purpose had been to pay devotion 'perhaps to both saints'.

The existence of the note had been long forgotten. I uncovered it by chance shortly after I had walked on my own the ancient pilgrim route of St. James, The Camino de Santiago, from southern France, over the Pyrenees and across the width of Spain to Santiago de Compostela.

The Mournes had a history too, much more recent than that chronicled by Harris. Everywhere I walked there was the evidence of man's work with the mountain's granite. The stones were cut and drawn from the mountainside to make fine buildings or city kerbs or, when the grain was right, for circular mill-stones. There were places too, where the granite was cut and used to build the Mourne Wall.

The granite workers cut and dressed the stone on site. Inside a small shelter there would be a fire, the heat raised by a bellows, an iron anvil and a shallow hollow in a stone called the 'fizz trough'. The workers made their own chisels, the iron heated in the fire, beaten on the anvil and tempered in the fizz trough.

When I was on my own I often explored these mountain sites where once men laboured long and hard. And sitting on a ledge at my ease where a man had grafted the day long for a living, I would search amongst the heather and find a chisel, left down for a moment and then forgotten.

Another John, John McCartan, a granite worker of Glasdrumman, became a friend. We met first at his work-shed at the fork in the lanes near the foot of Spence's Valley. John was self-employed. He cut kerb stones for export to the cities of the English Midlands. Well-meaning friends encouraged him to leave his hard graft by the lane side and go to work in the stone yard in the village.

"I can do without their diamond toothed saw," John would say, "When you're your own boss, the work can stop when you've made enough money to do for the next week." He would set the hammer down and grin.

"And that might be Wednesday afternoon or even Friday morning if there's a lot of celebrating to do at the week-end."

After a walk in the hills I would call to see John at his shed. He stopped work as usual when I arrived one day, but he was waiting for me, hardly able to contain himself.

John had the Mourne man's way of disguising a near-insult to make it sound like a compliment.

"You're a smart man," he said, "College educated. Read big books. Know all about everything."

I wondered what was coming. John had never been so animated before. It was obviously not a time for me to say anything. He rolled up his sleeve to the shoulder and put his arm against mine.

"Well if you're so smart, tell me this and tell me no more." He was pointing at his upper arm.

"Look at me," he said, "My arm's as thin as a stick and since before I was fourteen I've been banging away with this." He reached me his hammer, it had a 14 lb head on a 14" wooden shaft.

"Hold it out in front of your chest. You couldn't use this for an hour never mind a day. And look at the size of your arm. Sure you have shoulders like a Turkish wrestler and you've never done a day's work in your life".

I knew better than try to argue. Even the sporting side of the student and teacher life I had led, would have been of no account here as physical work, never mind mentioning my days as a physical education student. I played for time and told John that the big muscle of the upper arm, the biceps, the muscle-man's muscle, was not very efficient, that the real power came from another smaller muscle hiding below biceps. He was not impressed.

Then I had an idea.

"What about Popeye, John?" I said. John looked at me sideways to see if I was pulling his leg.

"Popeye the sailor man," I said, "Do you not remember Popeye's arms?"

I drew the shape in the dust with a twig, the thin upper arm and the bulging muscle below the elbow. I showed him where to hold my forearm to feel the muscle working as I used the hammer. He took the hammer in his right hand and felt his forearm bulge and tighten with his other hand.

"I told you, you were a smart man," he said, and it was still not a compliment, "It's hard to beat book learning."

His eyes narrowed. He continued to question me, trying not to show that he was too impressed, but with the air of a man who saw a few bottles of stout in the 'Popeye' theory. It would go down well in the bar of the Harbour Hotel, Newcastle, on a Saturday night.

"Now just go over that bit about Popeye again, Bert, to see if I have the right way of it."

It was one of many such conversations that John and I had at his workshed. Sometimes I even had the chance to quiz him. He needed a week to think out how he would explain it to someone as simple as myself, when I asked about the rule of thumb for cutting a stone to the required size from a great piece of rock.

Knowing John was an education. It was an education I would have missed had my interest in the Mournes been only in the mountains.

A few years later I went to one of the landmarks of the Mournes, the Hare's Castle, not one of the highest cliffs but perched so dramatically on a ridge above the bog it might have been a castle built by the Norman invaders.

It had been quarried for stone to build the Mourne Wall between 1910 and 1922. The wall was constructed to mark the boundary of the Belfast Water Commissioners property. It straddled fifteen mountains and enclosed 9,000 acres. At the time it was built some lovers of the Mournes were appalled at this intrusion into the natural environment. However, most of the enmity has receded with the passing years. Perhaps in time it will take a small place in history alongside Hadrian's Wall and the most illustrious wall of all, the Great Wall of China.

I sat in the sunshine amongst the piles of granite chips and the rejected blocks. The marks of chisels were still on the rock and I thought of the men who had worked here. No doubt that it had been a tough job. A long walk to get here every morning, long hours on the job, cold and wet weather, low wages, back-breaking physical work, they would all have combined to make this the very hardest of graft. I felt for them, but there would have been great crack too, stories, banter, jokes and the Mourneman's wily humour.

As I left I looked down at my feet and saw a sledge hammer almost hidden in the heather. I bent to pick it up and the wooden shaft crumbled to dust in my hands. Only the head was solid. It had been lying here since this section of the wall had been built, probably about 1920, left down for a moment and forgotten.

I brought the head home in my rucksac and fitted a stout, seasoned ash branch to it. Seventy years after it served the builders of the Mourne Wall it still serves as my sledge hammer. And I never lift it without thinking of the time it was used for real work.

JOHN'S HAMMER

The second hammer I found borne in by the tide.

The beach at Newcastle in County Down, is a three-mile strand of pale golden sand, fringed by sandhills which, for the first mile, hide what is meant to be one of the finest golf links in the world. Beyond the golf course is a nature reserve in the sand dunes which extends the whole way to the bar mouth of the inner, almost land-locked bay. The strand stretches the whole way from Newcastle to the village of Dundrum. The tide was out and on this gently-sloping beach it ebbs a long way out. Now it was on the turn.

The beach was empty of people on this afternoon, a bright cool day between winter and spring. I was running slowly back towards Newcastle with the best view of the town in front of me. At the far end the houses are perched above the harbour and the resort curves around the bay for over a mile to the grand Victorian facade of the Slieve Donard Hotel marking the near end.

A few sea-side towns in Ireland may have such a splendid setting but no other has a more spectacular back-drop. The ground to the south is steeply inclined on wooded slopes and rises abruptly to the summit of Slieve Donard, the highest mountain in the Mournes.

Donard is a great lump of a mountain, almost three thousand feet high but it is not the height of the peak which impresses. It is the closeness of its top to the shore and the sweep of its eastern flank down into the sea itself. Percy French must have often walked this beach and found it an inspiration for his art as well as his music.

Jogging at my pace is as much a mental relaxation as an act of physical exercise. Flocks of birds feeding at the edge of the water took to the air as I ran the tide line, wheeling back in formation to the same spot, calling their annoyance at being disturbed. My dog galloped through the shallows, running for fun.

Susie looks like an athletic black labrador, lighter in the hind quarters than that breed. Her dam was a pedigree labrador but the farm collie had jumped the fence into her pen and he was the sire. Susie loves to run, the faster the better, whether in the chase or just for the freedom of it.

14

On such a run the human takes time to adjust to the activity. Then it becomes obvious, in case we may have forgotten, that the body was designed for movement, perhaps not all frames designed for travelling at quite this speed, but for moving under its own power nonetheless.

After the first few minutes, perhaps ten or twelve in my case, the body's systems switch from 'sedentary mode' to 'activity mode'. Even the relatively fit feel some mild discomfort in the legs and chest until the switch occurs. Then, but only if the early pace is right for the individual, there is a dramatic change. All at once it seems as if, in such a natural setting, this is one of the most natural of human activities.

It is not merely some psychological trick of the mind but a physiological phenomenon. The body's physical systems have been activated as if by some hidden switch. Breathing becomes deeper and slightly quicker. Initial stiffness in the muscles or joints fades. Helpful chemical substances, of which adrenalin is perhaps the best known, are secreted into the blood stream, aiding the heart and lungs, one even easing the pain if we bruise a foot or scratch an arm. These secreted substances help too, to create a wonderful feeling of wellbeing.

The process works only to advantage if the surface and the pace for the individual are right. Too hard underfoot or too fast and there is discomfort or pain. It quickly becomes obvious that the game is not worth the candle. Too slow and the benefits may never become apparent. The range of speed of travel to suit the individual is wide - from steady walking for some - to running faster than would count as jogging for others.

This had been a good day for me. I had travelled about five miles at the right pace. The legs, lungs and heart all seemed to be working well. The sense of freedom and wellbeing lifted the spirits. Susie was enjoying herself.

And there it was in front of us, lying at the edge of the tide, wavelets so tiny they hardly broke over it, a hammer, a stone mason's short-shafted hammer. Susie beat me to it. She had a sniff and decided it was too heavy to make a chasing stick and left me to pick it up.

It was so like the hammer used by my friend John, the stone mason from Glasdrumman and now deceased that, by the time I reached home I was thinking of it as his.

In the early years of our friendship I was having a house built in Newcastle. Seeing in the estimates a sum for a fire place of my choice, I went to see John and asked him if he could make me a granite fireplace for the amount mentioned. I think it was probably £18 10 shillings.

Mourne men are not known for reckless displays of joy when something pleasing happens but John was delighted. He could hardly believe his luck or conceal his excitement at being asked to make such an item from stone.

"I thought people like you went in for wee fireplaces with shiny tiles and fancy grates." He grinned like a happy elf.

I said nothing but looked him over as if I was inspecting him for the job. He was a wiry build of a man, strong without bulk, slightly shorter than medium height, with a face which showed his every mood.

He was now all business. "We'd better get started. Before we do the design you and I will have to see a few stone fireplaces. It'll mean going to licenced premises. There are only three granite fireplaces around here and two of them are in pubs."

This was the work for John. This was the way life should be lived. The prospect of doing a job that was bound to be enjoyable was a gift from the fates.

We visited the pubs. John pronounced the Guinness good but he was unimpressed by the fireplaces. In the second establishment he scraped the grime off one of the side stones of the fireplace with a cardboard beer mat.

"There's why they don't clean it." He looked around to check that the publican was not within earshot. "If they did, it would show up that big crack."

He was right. I could see that the stone had split across its width.

"What happened?" I said, "Did it crack because the fire was too hot?"

"Not a bit of it." said John, "What kind of a fireplace would it be if you couldn't put a good fire on?

He ran his hand over the hearth, determined to educate me in the ways of granite working.

"The wrong man chose the wrong stone. That class of granite is too brittle and worse than that, it's the wrong grain."

I was impressed and tried to look so. We sipped our stout. This was the way to do business. Talk it over with the right person in the right place. Agree the idea and the function. Understand the material and the process.

Where had I read that before?

Right principles… Right purpose… Right discourse…

Take it a bit further and a whole way of life could be based on it.

John's instincts were making a pleasure of the project. We were beginning to see a work in stone which would satisfy both of us.

We met at his cottage a week later to design the fireplace. It was as if we both had the same picture of it in our heads. The top stone would be long and substantial with its front face finished roughly. It would be supported by two upright slabs with a smoother surface. The hearth would be long and wide with what was called a hammered finish.

Each of us then added an idea of our own. I suggested a small ledge to one side to give an asymmetrical effect. John liked this as just the distinctive touch we needed. He proposed to chamfer the front inside edges of the upright stones to let the heat radiate to the whole room.

It took less than fifteen minutes to design, draw and agree the plan.

"Fair enough." said John, "Now I have a stone I want you to see." He jumped to his feet and left the cottage at speed. I thought we were going around to the back to view a few pieces of granite but John was already on the track, heading up the mountain.

Ten minutes later we were beside a quarry on the slopes of Spence's Mountain. The view was over a great stretch of the coastal plain of Mourne between the townlands of the Ballagh and Ballymartin, with the fishing village of Annalong half way between the two.

The dwellings on the plain below were scattered as if at random. Each had its holding of land, more often small than large, its fields bounded by dry stone walls built from rocks dug from ground as it was cleared for cultivation. I know of no where else in Ireland where the dry stone walls are a match for those of Mourne.

The traditional wall built by the muscle of man has given way to walls made from much bigger stones set in place by the hydraulic power of the tractor. But the skills of choosing and placing the stones are as evident as ever and the new walls as good as the old.

Below us a track contoured the mountain, its passage through the stone walls served by distinctive iron gates painted red. The path and the gates mark the line of the underground pipe which carries the water supply from the Silent Valley Reservoir around the mountains and across the farmland of County Down to Belfast.

Nearby was a line of stone posts, thin slivers of granite which once formed a fence. In North-western Spain granite fences like this are common. In Northern Portugal, taller stone uprights support the vines which must be kept clear of the damp ground. The row of granite posts is still in place on the flank of Spence's Mountain, and is the only row of rock posts I know of in Ireland.

John stopped at a large boulder. It was about shoulder height, rounded, weathered, over two yards long at the base.

"What do you think of it?" he said proudly, laying a hand on the top of the huge rock.

What sort of comment did he want me to make? It would probably have been better to say nothing rather than state the obvious.

"It's a big lump of a rock " I said foolishly. John looked at me with the patience of a man used to dealing with the uninitiated, as if ignorance should be tolerated not mocked.

"Look at it." he said. "It's a beauty. Do you see that grain? Just what we need." I could see that he was anxious, hoping that I would like the stone. I nodded sagely, looking in vain for the slightest trace of grain on the weathered surface.

"Pepper and salt." he said, "That's what you call this class of granite. You'll see the black and white speckles better when I split it." We walked around the stone and I tried to agree with him completely without saying something stupid.

"Feel it." said John, "Not too brittle. It's the very stone for our job."

"How will you move it?" It was perhaps too obvious a question but I asked anyway, for it looked as if it must weigh tons.

John scrutinized my face to see if I was pulling his leg. Then he realised that I thought he intended to move it as it was.

"In bits." he said, "I"ll split it here and slipe them down to the house." This was better. I knew that a slipe was the wooden sledge used to move big stones over rough ground. My confidence grew. I felt the rock. I bent down and looked for the grain. I stepped out its length.

"This is it." I said, "I'll take your word for it."

John slapped me on the back and we went down the mountain to his cottage for a cup of tea.

Over the next fortnight John bought the boulder from the quarry owner for £5 and split it into manageable pieces using the 'plug and feather' method. This was the traditional technique and John was proud of the fact that he was one of the few who still used it. I had often watched him in operation.

With a hammer and chisel he would drill a row of holes on the line along which he wished the rock to split. He would place a blunt-nosed chisel called a 'plug' in each hole with two thin slivers of metal called 'feathers', one on each side. The 'feathers' enabled the 'plug' to be driven into the hole when hammered. When each hole was furnished with a 'plug' and 'feathers' he would move along the row, forward and back, tapping each 'plug' in turn until the rock split.

One Sunday morning I had a 'phone call from John.

"Can you come out to the house this afternoon?" He sounded worried, even distressed. It was not his usual form.

"What's wrong?" I said, "How's the fireplace coming on?"

"Oh, the fireplace is all right." said John, "It's the crowd of oul experts that gather every day to watch me trying to work at it. Every last one of them thinks he knows your mind better than me. For the first time in their lives they agree on something. They're sure that all I've done is to ruin good granite."

I arrived in the early afternoon and John came down the lane to meet me.

"I told them you were coming to view." he said, "So they're all here for an afternoon's entertainment."

The main problem was the large horizontal stone across the top of the fireplace. John and I had agreed that it should have a rough finish on the front. His critics were maintaining that he had cut one of the depressions too deeply and in so doing had completely ruined the stone.

When I reached the house there were about seven or eight elderly men, all retired granite workers. They had gathered to one side of the fireplace which John had erected beside his cottage. Some of them were known to me and we greeted each other.

"I hear you think John has made a great job of the fireplace." I said with a grin. They nudged at each other and avoided looking at me directly, like men who knew more than they were prepared to divulge.

"I'm sure it's not often a fellow has as much advice for a job as John has had for the past week. I'm very grateful to you for your help."

There were a few murmurings but no one was prepared to speak, as yet.

I looked at the big, speckled top stone and it was a marvellous piece of granite, five feet long and eleven inches deep.

"That's a magnificent stone." I said and fingered the rough depressions on the front. John looked at me nervously, this was the plane of contention.

"Look at the way he has it cut on the face." I said, "It's perfect. Exactly what I wanted."

The experts held their silence.

I pointed at the 'plug and feather' marks which I had asked John to leave on the front edge of the hearth and the ledge to one side.

"John wasn't keen to leave the plug and feather marks." I said, "But I insisted. This isn't a job cut to size with a diamond saw. What do you think of them?"

It was a direct question and out of courtesy, someone had to answer.

"I've never seen them left in before." said one of the older men tentatively, "But they look all right on the finished article." The others nodded in grudging agreement.

John was not to be placated.

"That's not what you were saying yesterday." he said. "You wouldn't believe that I was asked to leave them in."

"You stone men have always hidden your skills." I said, "In future John should leave the 'plug and feather' marks on some part of every job he does. It could be his trade mark."

They all smiled. In the past their skills would often have been underrated, not only by those who employed them, but by themselves too. And perhaps understandably so. If their finished work was appreciated by others on buildings and bridges and walls around great estates, that esteem would never have reached them. The price of their hire would have been the only tangible way they would have had of measuring the value society placed on their work. And low wages would have ensured a poor view of their trade.

My job was finished. John walked me back down the lane.

"Maybe that'll keep them quiet for a day or two." he said, "But I wouldn't bank on it. I'll have the fireplace ready to be installed next week. The sooner I get it away from here the sooner I'll have peace."

The builder paled when he saw the lorry arrive.

"It's massive!" was all he could manage to say. He stood with his jaw slack muttering to himself like a prayer, as if in the hope that repeating the phrase would make the problem of installing it easier.

It must be fairly rare for a fireplace to require special foundations but this one did. John came to see it in place and he was pleased almost beyond words. He took me aside, out of hearing of the workmen.

"I have a confession." he said, "The builder may know how to build a good house from bricks and blocks but he knows nothing about granite." He checked to see that we were not being overheard.

"He asked me to drill holes in the back of the stones and to fit in iron rods. They're called tie-bars. I've done that and he has cemented the tie-bars into the bricks to hold the fireplace against the wall."

It seemed a sensible technique and I said so.

"You're as bad as he is." said John patiently, "That fireplace will settle about an inch out from the wall over the next few years. If I had done exactly as ordered by him, it would have pulled the wall forward with it as it settled."

I must have looked concerned.

"Don't worry." John said craftily, "I've fixed the tie-bars so that they'll pull out from the back of the fireplace as it settles and your wall won't be affected."

He was right of course. Over the next few years the fireplace settled leaving a little space about an inch wide between top stone and the wall. He and I filled the gap with fire cement and the wall remained as true as ever. On the 'need to know' principle, we never told the builder. As John said.

"He won't be fitting many fireplaces like this one, but if he does the man who makes it will do as I've done."

A few years later, when he thought he had retired, John found himself involved in doing the stone work for the car park and coastal path at the Bloody Bridge near Newcastle. I went out to see the job and he showed me around.

"I took your tip." he said, "Every where you look you'll see I've left my trade mark."

Sure enough, the 'plug and feather' marks were there to be seen. It was the kind of memorial John would have wanted, not for himself, but for the trade that had been his life, and for all the stone men of Mourne.

HANK'S HAMMER

For a second time in a month I felt a great surge of freedom. I was walking uphill again amongst snow-buttressed peaks, my spirits soaring with me as the track rose.

We were in the Elburz Mountains of Northern Iran on a mountaineering expedition. The mullahs had yet to rise and bring the most dramatic Islamic revolution of the 20th century to what was once the ancient state of Persia. The Shah still sat on his Peacock throne and ruled his country with the power of a vast army and the cunning strength of secret police.

There were over thirty of us camped in a high valley in the finest range of mountains in the Elburz. To reach it we had spent two days climbing from the road-head to the foot of broken cliffs. The route to our valley lay up a steep gorge, cut through these cliffs by a river falling in a series of waterfalls. At this time of the year the cascades were ice-falls and the gorge choked by snow and rocks.

Our baggage train was 14 pack mules and their drivers. Half-way up the gorge we had to cross the icy torrent and the force of the water knocked over a mule and its boy driver. The other drivers saved the mule but the boy had to save himself. Although we lost valuable equipment, including a tent, the successful ascent of the gorge seemed a good omen.

We pitched our tents in a grassy valley hemmed in by high peaks. It was a wonderful place for a camp, and called Hazarchal, the valley of a thousand corries. Half a mile above our base a brown bear lived in a cave in a rocky promontory, as interested in us as we were in him.

When our climbers passed his home on the way to a peak, the bear came out to see them and would follow their footsteps. As they climbed the steep snow slope to the upper end of the Hazarchal, the distance between the bear and our friends would diminish quickly. The bear's snow climbing technique was much superior to that of the humans. But then he had his own built-in crampons.

Watching from the base camp with binoculars we took sides and cheered the contestants on their way. The rowdy crowd were on the side of the bear, but then mountaineers are like that, not always best pleased when

Base Camp in the Valley of a Thousand Corries

someone else is heading off to climb the peaks they see as theirs.

Above the ice-wall and once on the glacier the climbers disappeared quickly into a thin mist and the bear turned back. We could be sure it was not from tiredness that he was retreating. As leader of the expedition and having to take a responsible view, I tried to assure the more sensitive that the bear meant us no harm.

We had chosen a famous site for our camp. On a journey to the shores of the Caspian Sea, King Solomon had passed this way nearly three thousand years ago accompanied by the Queen of Sheba. The story still told in these parts tells how the King tried to encourage the Queen to share his bed.

His was the only tent and he had insisted that the whole entourage climb higher and higher into the mountains. The days were warm but each night was colder than the one before. The Queen held out until they reached the Valley of a Thousand Corries. There, the cold was so intense she joined the king in his tent. To mark the great event, the range became known as the Takht-i-Suleiman, the Throne of Solomon.

Late one afternoon five young Iranians arrived at our camp, tired and hungry. They had food and a storm lantern but no tent or cooking stove. I was preoccupied with a climbing group preparing to leave for a peak and had little time to talk to them. We made a stove available and cleared a space in the stores' tent for them to sleep.

At altitude water boils at a lower temperature than 100°C and their rice was still cooking late into the evening. They were on the way across the mountains, hurrying to their home village for a religious festival and travelling Solomon's Route.

Next morning they were away before any of us were up and I wished I had been less preoccupied with our own projects. We had shared an encampment which had been used for over three thousand years. But I had missed the chance to talk to them as a stranger in their land, a chance to listen for their echoes.

One of them left a note.

'Goodbye the people of the groups. We are very ashamed because we troubled you and we very thank you so you help our sleeping and our cooking the food and in fact to stay here. We must go to Taleghan very soon this morning. We hope to visit you after five or six day.

Yours affectionately
Mohammad Ali Ahdolmaleki'

I looked forward to their return but it was the last we saw of the five young Iranians. The pass they had headed for meant an ascent of a steep snow slope which, at the early hour of their attempting it, would have been icy and treacherous. When I walked up towards it later in the day I could see no sign of them except the line of their ascent. The other side, however, was presumably just as steep and descent can be more dangerous than ascent in such conditions. I worried for their safety.

One of our groups left a few days later to explore a remote area across the great ridge which hemmed-in our valley. A thousand years ago this corner of the Elburz Mountains was the home of the Assassins, a Persian sect which dominated the Middle-East from Persia to the Mediterranean. Their castles had been built in a remote mountain fastness, the Valley of the Assassins.

Their methods were simple. A message would be sent to someone in a position of power. If he failed to act as ordered a member of the sect would murder him, even though it meant losing his own life.

The sect prospered and extended its influence. Its fame spread to the East. The Crusaders brought tales of the prowess of the Assassins to Western Europe. Some would have it that the founders of the Knights Templar were influenced by this sect, apparently borne out by a curious similarity in the hierarchy and administration of the organisations.

Their memorial is the name we give to that form of killing, assassination.

In the 13th century a Mongol Army led by Hulaga Khan rode into Persia from the East and mounted a ferocious attack on the valley. The castles were sacked, the men and boys killed, the Assassins completely destroyed.

The cult of the Assassin is still with us. Their influence is extended by their acolytes. They wield their power from ghetto fastnesses. The creed is the same. Submit to our will or die.

Our party aimed to cross the ridges, perhaps the first to explore the valley from this direction, to see if there were remains of Assassin strongholds in the upper reaches. The BBC Television crew accompanying the Expedition were travelling with them and I joined the party to see them over the first crest.

Other climbing groups set off to climb the peaks. The base camp was almost empty. For the first time since we had arrived it was a place of ordered calm, quiet, relaxed, an idyllic mountain retreat.

In the history of mountaineering expeditions it is apparent that when the climbing teams have failed it is often because the climbers have been badly served by the base camp. An uninteresting site, poor water and sanitary arrangements, disorganised allocation of food and equipment, all stack the odds against success.

I had invited Arthur and Dick, a doctor and a lawyer, to manage our base camp. They were tall and lean and affected an exceedingly serious approach to their duties which kept even the most awkward of the climbers in his or her place. That the base camp worked so efficiently and was such a restful haven after a sortie was due to them. Their wry good humour calmed jangled nerves and eased the tensions which inevitably arise on an expedition.

One morning, and as all good leaders should do, I gave praise where it was due. Dick and Arthur exchanged smiles as if they had been waiting patiently for this moment for days.

"Thank you," said Arthur, "We're glad you're pleased," and he came straight to the point.

"Maybe this is a good time to remind you that you promised each of us a peak." It was the direct approach some medical men use when there is some uncertainty that the patient will take the news well.

It was not the way Dick would have put it. He would have sat me down with a cup of coffee and a wedge of cake. Probably it would have been a thick slice cut from one of the excellent Ormeau Bakery fruit cakes flavoured with Irish Whiskey which had been presented to us before we left. The control and patronage of such items was one of the few perks our base camp managers would admit to.

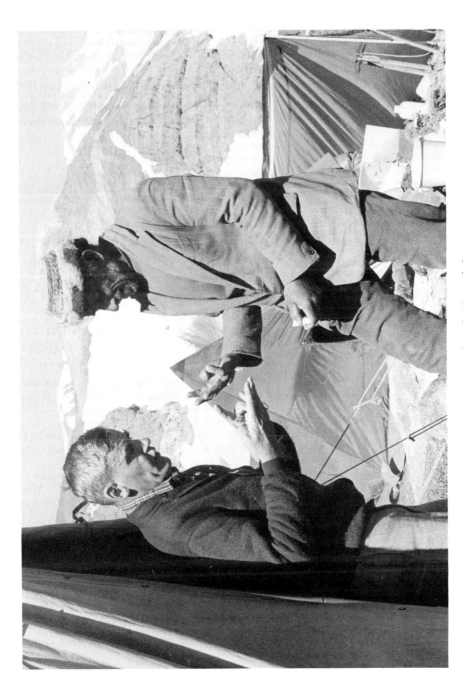

Dr Arthur at work in the Hazarchal

Dick would have raised the subject casually and then convinced me that it was a climb I could hardly wait to do. Stalling for time, I said as much and Arthur laughed.

"But he didn't get his oar in first." There was a logic in that, that even Dick, the fearless debater in the most intimidating arenas, dare not challenge.

Arthur and I left early next morning for his peak. The track across the scree soon disappeared under snow as we climbed. This was the route the Iranians had used and we could follow their foot prints.

At the foot of the pass we found the ruins of what had once been a rest house. Long before King Solomon's time, the track would have been one of the most important routes between the ports of the Caspian Sea and the interior. The road through the mountains which we had used was relatively new and since Solomon's journey, holy men, travellers and traders' caravans would have passed this way.

The ruined rest house would have been part of a chain of stopping places. On our way up to the Hazarchal we had paused for tea at the next in the chain. It was near enough to the road head to be still in use.

Beside the ruins was a rock mound, perhaps twelve feet long, by six feet wide, with an upright stone at the south side. It could only have been an ancient grave.

As expected, the snow leading to the pass was frozen but the footprints on the line of ascent made the going easier for us than it would have been for the young Iranians.

At the crest of the pass we looked over and saw the icy slope on the other side, curving down to the south. This was the route Solomon's caravan would have climbed on the way to the Hazarchal. Nearly three thousand years have passed. We think now that we live in a different world. But these mountains would have changed little in such a short time in the earth's history. Some erosion of the terrain, some small climatic changes perhaps but the prospect before us would have been virtually the same as that revealed to Solomon and Sheba and their great band of followers when they reached this place.

Far below our tents were barely discernable, tiny flashes of orange and green amongst patches of snow and rocky outcrops. It was the only good site in the whole of the Hazerchal. It must have been the same place used by that royal caravan and by travellers, pilgrims and mule trains for over thirty centuries.

Sometimes we share the privilege of such a contact with history without even a pause to feel its resonance. Casually, finger at the right page in the guide book, camera at the ready, we glance at a wonder of the natural world or some famed or fabled manifestation of man's art or artefacts and speak in momentary awe. Perhaps the awe is tinged with nagging disappointment at money or time spent to visit somewhere not quite as thrilling as the last great site on a crowded itinerary.

Arthur and I were moved to silence to be in such a place. We drank from our waterbottles and shared the biscuits. The plod up the scree and snow to the summit seemed shorter and easier than the ascent to the pass.

Standing on the summit of Lashkeram, height 4,300 metres, about 14,100 feet, Arthur was a happy man. It was his first big mountain and all the worry and hard work of keeping over thirty people fit and well must have seemed worth the effort.

For me it was another moment of freedom. Scattered across this vast spread of mountains were the expedition groups and the BBC film crew. Out of contact with them there was nothing I could do to influence their progress. For this brief pause, I could almost let go of duty.

Arthur and I shook hands and sat down to look at the world spread out before us. We were in no hurry and there was no need for conversation. Such a moment could never be stolen from us.

Four ravens occupied a near-by ridge to keep an eye on us. Much further away an eagle and a vulture left almost the width of the valley between them as they soared above the scree.

We were a long time on the summit as if, like the ravens, we were reluctant to give up our perch.

Back at base camp Dick was busy with in-coming groups, allocating food boxes. He needed our help. Groups returning to base were entitled to some luxury items like spices, herbs, cake, custard powder and ready-mixed flour for making wheaten bread, pancakes and potato bread. Allocating these required alertness and the strictest control.

The next surge of freedom came much later. Our time in the mountains was running out when Dick and I set off one afternoon. We planned to climb Alam Kuh, the highest peak in the range, the next morning. Our chosen route was the way by which Sir Douglas Busk had made the first ascent in the nineteen thirties.

Some distance from our camp we turned into a narrow valley and

Dick at Base Camp

followed a glacier to a lateral moraine. Above us to the north was the ridge which rose steeply to the summit of Alam Kuh and by which Busk had climbed the peak.

We now needed a place where we might bivouac safely and relatively comfortably for the night. I stopped amongst the rocks of the moraine beside the glacier and took off my rucksac.

"Is this it?" Dick looked down at the sharp stones at his feet.

I looked up to check that we would be safe from stone fall and muttered assent.

Dick was scuffling the rocks about with a toe.

"Lying on this will be like trying to sleep on a bed of nails."

"Don't worry," I said, "It's all in the mind. Fakirs can do it. You'll never feel a thing."

Dick has the kind of mind which not only enables him to tell what you are about to say but also what you are thinking. It will have been of no small importance in his professional life and useful too, in dealing with tricky friends. This time however, I thought I might have the advantage of him.

"You see, Dick," I was at my most reassuring. "On a moraine like this there is always fine gravel and sand under the rocks. We move the top layer and underneath there will be a very comfortable bed."

He shook his head. "You make these things up as you go along," he said, unaware that a few yards before we stopped, I had scraped the stones back with my foot just to check that there would be gravel after all.

We made two depressions, side by side, like shallow graves. The excavated stones formed a low wind break around the edge. Our plastic survival bags covered the gravel and formed a lining for the bivouac. Then we placed the layer of foam which gives insulation and a little comfort from the hip to the shoulder. The down sleeping bags, unrolled on top, expanded to fill the space.

The cool of evening was turning quickly to the cold of the night and we had supper, sitting up in the comfort of the sleeping bags. This was the place to see the stars, high in the mountains under a clear eastern sky. A satellite, like a moving star, rose from behind one ridge and in a few moments had disappeared behind another.

We talked quietly, seriously, with more silent pauses than words, the day's banter finished. My rucksac felt like the perfect pillow.

At first light we were both awake. Leaning on one elbow, still in his sleeping bag, Dick lit the stove to boil water for tea.

Twenty minutes later we were climbing the frozen snow towards the ridge. Unless the slope is very steep, the ice axe is held by the head and the steel point on the bottom of the shaft driven into the snow to give security, as the feet kick their way upwards. The sun had yet to rise above the rim of our horizon but the exercise of the ascent warmed us.

At the rock ridge we met the sun and paused for our first rest. At this point we joined the route of Busk's first ascent. It was a narrow, airy ridge, curving upwards towards the peak. The valley floor on our right was much lower than the one we had climbed from, a sheer drop of perhaps three thousand feet.

Some time later we reached the first of a series of 'gendarmes', rocky pinnacles on the ridge which barred the way to the top. While we rested, I produced a climbing rope from my rucksac. Dick was not anticipating any roped climbing so I had kept it hidden in my sac, on the principle that there was no need for him to know, unless we had to use it.

This was the place where the guide accompanying Sir Douglas Busk refused to rope up for safety. After the strongest protests, which were cheerfully ignored by Busk, the guide followed reluctantly. No doubt he was spurred on by the fear of being left alone on the ridge, when Busk proceeded up the rocks without him.

"What's the rope for?" asked Dick rhetorically and perhaps with less finesse than usual.

"This is where we tie on," I said, as casually as I could manage. "It's not difficult, the rock's just a bit loose."

"Loose!" said Dick, pretending to be indignant at the mountain's lack of consideration for our safe passage. "The whole mountain is disintegrating under our every step." He settled himself against the rock and gave me an encouraging smile. "I'll just wait here. You can pay my respects to the summit and I'll sit in the sunshine until you come back."

"It's not as easy as that," I said gently. "We may not be coming down this way. Busk says there is an easier way down."

"Good old Sir Douglas," said Dick as he rose to his feet. "Where would we be without that grand class of English diplomat-adventurers.?"

We roped up and climbed carefully, working our way up the ridge. We rounded the first two gendarmes, moving one at a time and scrambled over another. Quite quickly we were at the foot of the rocky outcrop which was the top of Alam Kuh.

It was time to pause and gather our strength. The climb had been long and strenuous but we were nearly there. There was no chance of this being a false summit, as often happens near the top of a mountain. The peak was just above and all around the rock fell steeply away. This was Dick's first big mountain and I thought of a way to mark the moment for him.

"Your lead," I said and followed him up the last few feet to the summit.

There was just enough room on the very topmost rock for us to sit down and open our rucksacs. The peak was at a corner in two ridges. To the north there was a sheer precipice dropping over two thousand feet into the Alam Chal Valley.

Joe and Raymond would climb this fantastic face in the next few days by a dangerous and difficult route. It became the most spectacular of the Expedition's climbing achievements. Teddy and Rory climbed the peak too, by another dramatic line, now known as the Ulster Route. In all, fourteen members of the expedition made the ascent of Alam Kuh by six different routes.

But on this day Dick and I were on our own, at almost 16,000', on the top of the highest peak in this part of the range. Only thirty miles away lay the Caspian Sea and its luxuriant coastal plains fringed with woods. We had seen that view earlier but now it was hidden from view. Below us the cloud had formed covering the valley floors. Only the highest peaks poked their tops through to the clear air above. The cloud's texture in its upper reaches was like teased-out sheep's wool. A little lower the white mass looked solid enough to walk on.

We left the peak knowing each other better in ways neither of us could have articulated. The cloud below us dispersed and we began the descent of the ridge.

Something caught my eye amongst the rocks at the upper end of the valley in which we had bivouacked. It looked like a body wedged between the boulders. We had to investigate and I found a way down the steep slope on rubble weathered from the ridge above.

Reaching the valley floor I stood up on a rock to locate the spot. Once there, it was a relief to find it was not a body but a rucksac jammed in a crevice between two boulders and looking like a man's back. We searched in a wide sweep for signs of a camp or other remains but there were none. The rucksac had just emerged from the previous winter's melting snow. It had been here for at least a year, perhaps much longer.

The sac disintegrated as I tried to open it. Inside was a duvet and an anorak soaked with water. Both ruined. There was a water bottle, a pair of ex-army crampons, a tin which appeared to have once held cheese, and a tin of Ovaltine tablets. But the most interesting item was a climber's piton hammer with a great curved spike at one end of the head.

There were no papers, nor was there evidence of the owner except on the piton hammer. On the shaft, burned into the wood was the word 'HANK'.

Who Hank was, I never discovered. Had he dropped the rucksac from the ridge? From where we found it that would have seemed most unlikely. Had he perished with it? If so, it would not be surprising that we failed to find his remains. Bears and wolves are efficient scavengers and we had seen both in the past few weeks.

Except for the piton hammer, we buried the remains of Hank's possessions and covered the hole with a mound of rocks. I brought the hammer back with me in my sac. Later I checked with the Iranian Mountaineering Association, but Hank did not appear in their records.

A Horseman in
Solomon's Mountains

If he had survived the mountains, Hank and I might meet sometime and I could give him back his hammer. As we reached the end of the expedition, the finding of Hank's rucksac and its contents, which represented his life support system in this terrain, seemed a sharper symbol of time spent in these mountains than a great peak climbed.

In the same way that the sledge hammer had connected me with the Mourne Mountains and a particular moment in their history, finding Hank's hammer connected me with the Throne of Solomon and the people of this area in a way that no mountaineering achievements could ever do.

As we reached base camp the film crew had already set up their equipment and were waiting, camera running. Jeremy was the interviewer, then a rising star, now a famous and fearless interrogator. He was ready with the mike.

Dick did the talking... Yes, we had climbed Alam Kuh... A wonderful peak... Magnificent views... No, it wasn't too difficult... We hadn't needed to rope up until we met the gendarmes on the ridge...

I stood in the background and smiled. The interview was going smoothly but only as expected.

"I thought you weren't a rock climber," said Jeremy sensing an opening.

Dick smiled the smile of a counsel who knows the case is won and needs only a few silvern words to seal the victory.

"Like hanging, Jeremy," he said, as if imparting a confidence, "Learning to rock climb at 14,000 feet concentrates the mind wonderfully."

We didn't tell them about Hank's hammer. That tale could wait.

CASTELGANDOLFO

It was the first time any of them had pitched a tent for real. They had practised in the school grounds, but that was only playing at camping. Now we were on the mountain, an hour and a half's walk from the nearest road, high enough to see out over miles of County Down countryside. And we were here for the night.

It would have been impossible not to have been infected by their enthusiasm. These fourteen-year-old boys were from the villages and farms that we overlooked, but none of them had ever camped or walked amongst these mountains. It was the adventure of their lives and they had been looking forward to it for weeks.

Although the food and equipment had made the back packs heavy, the walk up had been relatively easy. At this early stage in their lives, those who lived on farms were already accustomed to hard physical work. We were in one of the two great corries of the Mournes, the Pot of Legawherry, under Slieve Commedagh and Slieve Corragh.

Many of them could see this steep-sided, flat-floored cauldron from their homes. In winter the snow streaked the cliffs that were its sides and the white caps of the two peaks above made its shape one of the most dramatic features in the range.

From our vantage point they could pick familiar land-marks close to home but now seen in miniature from on high.

The eight of them erected their three tents with a degree of concentration and application that would have staggered their parents and the teachers we had left behind. I pitched the tent that Rex, the other teacher and I would share, and he and I wandered amongst them offering advice and encouragement. But as I watched, I worried.

Our camp was well placed to one side of the Pot. We were hemmed in at the back and sides by cliffs, scree and steep heather slopes. The floor of the corrie was flat. A stream, fed by trickles from clefts in the cliffs, meandered past our tents and tumbled down over the lip of the Pot into the much broader valley below.

It was not the site of our camp which bothered me, it was the three little tents being erected by the boys. Pools of camping equipment, provided by education boards for school and youth club use, were still in the future. A few schools and youth organisations arranged walks and camps but the great interest by educational bodies in the outdoors had not yet begun.

The boys' tents now being pitched had been borrowed from family friends. One was white and the other two a very faded shade of palest green. They looked so flimsy, so fragile. Their canvas sides fluttered in the breeze. It was hard to believe that they might repel the lightest of showers, never mind heavy rain.

My own tent was home-made from the very finest light-weight Willesden canvas. It was a half-pyramid shape, made to a design from a book on wilderness camping which I had adapted to fit my own ideas. I knew it would keep out the worst of the weather but, if the other tents failed, it would only be big enough to shelter four of us.

The weather forecast had been good and the afternoon bright and dry. Now the clouds were rushing in from the west and the first spots of rain fell. The shower became a rain storm. The wind swirled into the Pot in great gusts, snatching at the shelters. We retreated to our tents to sit it out. Half an hour later it was raining steadily and I emerged to see how the boys were coping.

In each little tent there was the same picture of gloom. The water was dripping in from myriad leaks as if the pores of the canvas were open and it was merely slowing the fall of the rain. The boys were sitting in their waterproofs trying to shelter their bedding, soaked and miserable.

I called them all to my tent and opened its doors so that as many as possible could shelter in its lee.

"I think you all know," I said it as gently as I could, "That we can't stay here as planned." None of them looked at me. Their heads were down. Had boys been allowed to cry in such circumstances, some of them would have shed tears.

"We still have a choice," I said. "We need to pack up and leave here. But we can either go home or we can walk across the mountains to a little cottage I know on the other side."

The heads came up and eight young faces looked at me.

"Don't take us home, master," one of them said. The school was in Castlewellan, and the country children still called the male teacher 'master'. It sounded like 'maister', and was of of course, short for 'school-master'.

"Not on the first day, master. Don't take us home on the very first day."

"It's a long way to the cottage," I said. "And the first stretch is up that slope." I pointed to the side of Commedagh. It was a thousand feet of the steepest walking in the Mournes. "And when we get to the top, it'll take hours to walk across the mountains."

They looked to Rex for support. "You ask him, master. Get him to take us to the cottage." His face lit up like theirs.

"Let's go to the cottage, Bert," he said. "You lead on and we'll be with you every step of the way."

It was a show of confidence that could not be ignored but I needed more.

"The cottage is not much of a place."

"That doesn't matter." Rex was now the spokesman "It'll be better than this." Now the boys had a champion, they gave him their full support.

"You tell him master," they said. "Don't let him take us home to-night."

"The wet tents will feel as heavy as lead."

"That's O.K." they said, "We can carry them."

"You won't get your meal until midnight."

"That's all right. We're not hungry."

Rex knew what I was up to. It would be a tough walk and I needed more than agreement. I needed them to be committed.

"This crowd won't let you down," he said. "They'll do it."

We packed up the sodden tents and lashed them to the outsides of the rucksacs to keep them separate from the spare clothes and bedding. The boys were in great spirits now. We crouched in a little circle for shelter and ate bread and jam to keep us going. Dinner would be much later that evening.

It was raining steadily as we started up the slope. I knew a route which would allow us to avoid the rock faces. We climbed slowly and entered a grey cloud which had settled on the back of the mountain. The cliffs behind the Pot were split by narrow gullies and weathered to form towers and spires like the Castles of Commedagh on the other side of the ridge. The mist streamed around these rocky walls and pillars and later the boys told me that they thought I was leading them by a secret route, up through the very middle of the cliffs.

We stopped at the bottom of a short scramble up rock and scree and

Rex and I saw them safely to the top. On the shoulder of the mountain we reached a narrow ledge between the cliff and the Mourne Wall and paused in the shelter of the wall for a moment. The boys could have been forgiven for thinking they were travelling through the most rugged mountains in the world.

I told them that the next stretch would be along the Brandy Pad and that this was the weather the smugglers prayed for, when they were crossing the hills with their loads of contraband. They were less likely to be caught by the Excise Men in the rain and mist.

On a fine day this is a good route, one of the most pleasant hill walks in the country. There are splendid views of nearly every peak in the Eastern Mournes. The long summit ridge of Slieve Binnian is on the skyline to the south. During World War 2, American soldiers billeted along the coast called it 'Convoy Mountain'. Its rocky tors reminded them of ships in convoy on their hazardous voyage across the Atlantic.

The cliffs of Ben Crom, the stooped peak, lean over a reservoir shaped like a narrow mountain tarn. The ridge that leads across Cove Mountain to Slievelamagan, 'climbing by creeping mountain', begins at Slieve Beg. As its name suggests, Beg is the smallest peak, but its cliffs are amongst the most impressive in the range.

They are split by a great fissure, the Devil's Coach Road, down which the headless coachman is meant to drive the devil's coach. If you doubt the connection, read Richard Rowley's poem 'Patsy the Pedlar'. In it Patsy tells of Saint Michael relaxing his vigilance one night here in the Mournes and…

> He forgets that under the mountain,
> In a mighty cave in the rocks,
> Oul' Nick is chained wi' a hand-forged chain
> To a couple of granite blocks;

But the Devil escapes from his incarceration in the cave in the Mournes. As Patsy says,

> He's broken the chain, an' jeuked the guard.
> An' given a flop o' his wing,
> An' he's aff careerin' across the world,
> Upsettin' everything.

and Rowley has Patsy the Pedlar recounting the tale as the reason for World War 2.

On this wet, misty evening it was easy to believe.

Usually in the hills I would have wanted the boys to share the lead, taking their turn to set the pace and find the way. But on this evening I led from the front and kept the pace slow and steady. The boys followed in close single file and Rex brought up the rear.

The line moved as if we were roped together, with each one towing the one behind. In good conditions it can be difficult to keep a lively group of boys together in the hills. On this occasion there was no need to impose any form of discipline, the mountain and the weather dictated their own terms.

We reached the Mourne Wall at a col on the south side of Slieve Donard and for half a mile we walked the broad, flat top of the wall to avoid the Bog of Donard. As darkness slowly enveloped the hills, we left the wall and found our way down the Spence's Valley to the cottage.

It was set into the hillside, its back to the worst of the weather. I saw its roof's dark shape appear silhouetted against the lighter shade of the sea 800 feet below.

"Is that it?" The boy who asked could hardly bear to do so in case he was wrong.

I was as relieved as they would be, when I told them that we had arrived.

"Well done! You've made it. Welcome to Castelgandolfo."

Inside we lit an oil lamp and two or three candles and left our kit against the back wall. The boys looked around the two rooms in silence. They took it in turns to climb the wall ladder, peeping through the trap door to see the sleeping loft. The fire place was a cottage hearth with an open grate and a high mantelpiece. There was a traditional 'crane', the pivoted metal bar with hooks, to hang pots over the fire.

There was both dry kindling and logs, it being a matter of honour between those of us who used the cottage to ensure that, at the end of each visit, the makings of a fire were left for the next occupants. In minutes the fire had the place warm and the steam rising from damp clothes.

"I thought you said it wasn't much of a place." One of the boys was indignant. "This is a great house. You shouldn't be running it down."

He was not able to see me smile. I thought that this was the perfect mountain haven, but better him praising it, than me.

We pooled the food and cooked on two Primus stoves and the open fire. The eating was a serious business and undertaken almost without conversation. Even though they were so quiet, I knew the boys were enraptured to be here. Their few words said it all.

The effort of the walk had been worth it. The comfort of this simple cottage was the reward. It was in such contrast to the miserable prospect at the beginning of the evening, they felt it to be the perfect refuge in the hills.

A few years later, at the end of a long climb through a white mist, I found my first Alpine hut high above the glacier, almost hidden in a snow drift. I shared that feeling and remembered the boys from the school in Castlewellan.

They came to life as the meal ended and wanted me to tell them about the cottage. The fire was going well. The heat drove us back and we sat in

Castelgandolfo

a semi-circle almost as far back from it as the walls would allow. I told them how we came to have the place.

The cottage was on the open mountain side, about twenty minutes walk from the nearest lane and in the valley above John McCartan's work shed. One day, on the way down from a peak, I stopped to look it over, and when I reached John's shed, I asked him how we might rent it. He took me to meet the owner, another John, John Carr and it was agreed that we could have it for £10 a year.

Two weeks later Arthur and I signed the lease. I knew that a number of my friends would be interested. We had often discussed renting a disused cottage and fixing it up as our place in the hills. Most of the group were from Ballymoney in North Antrim. I had taught there, at Dalriada School, on my first job. With a fellow teacher, Bill, we had arranged walking and camping trips to the Mournes. Although I was now teaching in Castlewellan and the Dalriada boys I knew had left school, the interest in the outdoors had kept some of us in contact.

"I'm glad to see you've made it weather proof." John Carr met Arthur and me as we came down after fixing the door and putting in new windows. He wanted to tell us that he was pleased to see the place being used. "Once the door goes, the east wind can blast in through the opening and blow the roof off from the inside."

"I'll tell you now, your rent won't be raised in my lifetime." We shook hands again on the deal.

In the Mourne area, when a tenant improved a rented cottage, the landlord would sometimes say that the place was needed for a son returning home from England. It was a device to encourage the tenant to offer a higher rent, rather than a need to accommodate a relative.

John was telling us that he would treat us differently.

Jack Newell, who lived on the opposite side of the river to John McCartan, welcomed us to the valley. He too, was pleased to see that the cottage would not become another derelict building on the mountain. His tales of the farmers and stone workers of the nineteen twenties and thirties were the fascinating folk history of the Spence's Valley.

A year after we had signed the lease the cottage became the place where my friends from Ballymoney and I could meet when we were walking and climbing in the hills. The boys listened intently as I told them how we had worked on the building.

Davy, who later became my first voluntary instructor when I was involved in mountaineering training, and Ian, who is still a walking companion, had been pupils at the school in Ballymoney. The three of us washed the soot and cobwebs off the inside of the roof so that we could use the loft to sleep in. Gilmour, James and John helped us dig out the great pile of sheep dung in the kitchen.

Bill, his brother Bertie and Rex took charge of technical jobs like making cupboards and laying the floor from pavement slabs. The slabs were heavy and we all helped carry them on improvised pack frames, from the head of the lane on the far side of the river.

The boys admired the work and wished they had been there to help. Then one of them said.

"You called the place Castle something when we arrived."

I smiled, remembering our first overnight here.

"The first time we came up to spend the night, there was a board tacked up in place over the door with one word on it, as if it was the name of the place. It said CASTELGANDOLFO." None of these boys would have known the significance of the name.

I explained that the next day I had met John McCartan and he had laughed as soon as he had seen me.

"You didn't know the place was called Castelgandolfo," he said grinning with delight. "But I'm sure even you have heard that it's the name of the Pope's summer palace."

"The old bachelor who used to live at the cottage was very holy. He was always the first to the church door for mass and the last away, so we called him 'the Pope'." John was enjoying telling me the story. "Then 'the Pope' was left a house further down the valley. So he lived in it during the winter and only went up to the cottage for the summer."

He paused to let me guess the next part of the story.

"It could be raining or blowing a gale but the first night any of us saw a light at the cottage window, the word would go round the townland. Summer's here. It must be. The Pope's gone up to his summer palace."

Bill and I had brought the Dalriada boys to camp in the Mournes near here and as my mountaineering work drew me away from the cottage, he began to spend more time there. His presence and his work on the place kept this disparate group together.

Over the years, and with occasional help from his friends, particularly Ian, the skilled man for tricky pipe work, who had sensibly returned to work in Northern Ireland, Bill made a great series of improvements. The Ballymoney school began to use the place as a base for their outdoor activities. My work changed and I was able to use it more.

Then an opportunity to buy the cottage arose and Bill, Ian and I became the owners.

Although it has changed much from the simple cabin that offered shelter to the boys from the Castlewellan School, it pleases me to see it in the same use after almost forty years.

A year ago I parked my car to walk across a ridge to the cottage. Standing near the parking area was Sam, who had been in that Castlewellan School group. Since then the school has closed and Sam has twice been seriously injured in road accidents. He can drive but is no longer able to walk any great distance.

He pointed at the ridge. "It's over there, isn't it?" as anxious to be right as the boy was that dark night we arrived at the cottage in the rain.

"That's it," I said, "The cottage called Castelgandolfo. It was a hard walk that night but we made it."

"I remember," said Sam, who had found it hard to remember. "I remember it now."

THE EVANGELIST, THE NURSERYMAN AND THE MAN FROM THE MINISTRY

There were three of us in a small tent high in the hills. Each one was as keen to spin a tale as the other two together, so there was nothing for it, even for me, but to sit back and listen.

It was one of those occasional winters, when the wind from the north brings a period of such severity, that it comes to be known, unimaginatively but accurately, as 'The Big Snow'. The Mournes were transformed. They looked like a new range, higher and more sheer, as if the cold had forced them upwards. The valley floors were deep in dry, powdery snow, which the gentlest breeze could lift and send skimming. The mountain slopes were plastered white, the ice on the steeper flanks polished by the wind, dully gleaming.

Slieve Donard had an ice dome as a summit, hiding all its features except its humped back of a sky-line and the cliffs of Eagle Rocks. The sharper outlines of Slieve Bernagh and Slieve Binnian were like Alpine peaks, with long iced faces sweeping upwards to their summit tors, changed in colour from granite grey to black against the lightening sky.

Hanging from the north-west shoulder of the second highest peak in the Mournes, Slieve Commedagh, the witches' cauldron of the Pot of Legawherry, could have been in Arctic Norway. The two-day blizzard which brought the snow had blocked the roads to Belfast and three of us had decided to pitch a tent in the Pot, where I had planned to camp with the boys from the Castlewellan school some years before. This time we hoped to spend a few days learning about deep winter in the Mournes.

Brian and I left Newcastle in the afternoon. As we reached the Spinkwee River, a white mist settled on the backs of the mountains and slipped down the valley to the lower slopes and the forest. Our boots squeaked on the powdered snow. There was no sign of the Spinkwee River. The snow had drifted and the river was buried deep, in places perhaps six feet under the crust. The mist hid every other feature of this once familiar terrain. It was as if we were climbing here for the first time.

At one point Brian stopped and rummaged in his rucksac for a compass. To our amazement it showed that, in this valley which we knew so well, we were now travelling in the wrong direction. Having entered and walked up the valley on its true left flank, we had veered left and crossed below the lip of the Pot still climbing. We were now walking out of the valley on the right flank, still ascending, of course.

It meant turning around to go in exactly the opposite direction. We laughed to cover the sheer embarrassment of it, and made our way into the Pot. The tent had been specially designed for conditions such as these. When we put it up, it seemed far more secure and comfortable than we had the right to expect of such a light canvas and alloy structure.

Philip had in his charge one of the foremost plant nurseries in these islands. In weather like this he had his greenhouses to check and he joined us in the late afternoon. We enquired about his journey through the mist. There had been no difficulty, he assured us, he had simply followed our foot-steps in the snow. They had led him directly up the valley to the door of the tent. We let him into our secret. Philip was not one to be discomfited by such a circumstance, but telling him of our little deviation eased our embarrassment.

Brian too, worked as a horticulturist, though some might have said that plants were his hobby and mountains his real life. There is advantage in taking to the mountains in the company of such professionals. They know about plants. They can find the most tiny and beautiful flowers hidden on apparently barren scree. They can fascinate the layman with the whole seed, breed and generation of some tiny, hitherto untroubled species, growing away as hard as it can in a sheltered cleft. Such glimpses of true beauty help the mountaineer make a friend of the mountain.

There was another, much less obvious, but equally significant advantage. I discovered that they knew about shelter from the wind.

My companions, the nurseryman and the man from the ministry, were a powerful combination of learning and experience. To a casual observer it could have appeared that they were remarkably similar men, of medium height, wiry build, easy of conversation, surprisingly interested in their fellow humans as well as plants. But watching them move on a mountain or living with them in high places revealed deeper truths.

One skipped across the rough slopes like the roe deer in Solomon's Song, leaping on the mountains of spices. Such was the intensity of his interest in say, a plant or a hill or a piece of music that he could stop a self-confessed philistine mountaineer in his tracks.

A few years before we had shared our first Alpine climb. For him it fulfilled an ambition born in the desert in North Africa in the worst days of World War 2. When we reached safe ground on the descent, he felt that I might not appreciate the emotion of this ambition fulfilled. I may not have been able then, to wear my heart on my sleeve as he did, but I understood.

The other walked at the steadiest of mountain paces, a pace so highly regarded that, in high mountains, hard men and even hard women, were content to fall in behind him, to make sure that they could keep going until the day's end. His was the kind of wit that could involve and hold companions in thrall no matter how long the journey. He and I would later share on Kaldi Dag in Turkey the hardest climb I ever faced.

Both of them gave conversation a good name.

On this evening they decided that I needed to be educated on the subject of shelter. I should have been able to guess what to expect.

The wind freshened and with the prospect that the blizzard might return, it was obvious that shelter would help our tent survive the night. Philip and Brian took charge and under their joint instructions we built a curved snow wall for protection.

They supervised, discussing the technicalities and allowed me to help with the physical work of building.

The wall began to take solid shape and was soon as high as the ridge of the tent. My friends knew that, when the wind hit the wall, its flow would roll over the top and strike the tent with even greater force. They explained that this type of turbulence is a common problem for those who garden in breezy areas.

Improbable as it might seem, the cunning gardener protects the plants from the wind with netting wire. The theory is that the wire slows down the moving air without the risk of the fierce turbulence which would be caused by a solid structure.

We dug holes in our beautiful curved snow wall with ice-axes, giving it an eroded, care-worn look, which made it seem as if it had been in place for years. There was much debate about the most effective size and shape of the holes. By now I felt well enough qualified by my building experience to join in. They paid me no attention, so I carved holes in artistic shapes, square in cross-section, triangular, heart-shaped.

The job done, it was passed as satisfactory by the experts. But if they noticed my special touches they passed no remark. We removed our outer clothing and boots and eased ourselves into the tent.

Unlike the manual work of building a snow wall, cooking in a tent is regarded as highly skilled and thus a much sought after task. I managed to corner the food and the two stoves. From such a position of strength I appointed Brian as my assistant and warned Philip to keep out of our way at the back of the tent.

It was a simple meal. Mugs of potato soup were followed by a stew made from tinned meat, onions and carrots and thickened with potato powder. There was no use in their pretending otherwise, they enjoyed that meal. For twenty minutes there was no conversation, the silence broken only by involuntary noises of appreciation and the wind skittering across the back of the tent.

Once the meal was over, Philip pushed his way forward from the back. I lay on my sleeping bag and let him commandeer the cooking position and the stove. He began to brew up a hot drink and Brian told us a tale of coincidence.

That summer the three of us were due to go to south-eastern Turkey as part of the Ulster Expedition to the Taurus Mountains. We had been speculating about the peaks and the villages. Discussing what we had each been able to learn from books.

Brian's story began with him driving home one dark night and giving a lift to a woman with a small suitcase. She proved to be an evangelist travelling to speak at a mission meeting. Trying to defend himself against the missionary's best efforts to save his soul, he was soon telling her of his interest in mountaineering and the planned trip to Turkey.

The missionary could hardly have been more pleased. She had crossed southern Turkey by road the previous summer and had seen the Taurus Mountains. She had used the pass, the Cilician Gates, which St. Paul himself had used to cross the southern flank of the range.

We listened enthralled as he remembered her descriptions of the snow-capped peaks and the people. It was as if she had been sent to tell us that the Taurus would be all that we hoped it would be.

Philip could hardly contain himself. He too had been driving home one wet night when out of the darkness of the road-side hedge a suitcase had appeared in his headlights. It was brandished by an arm and followed quickly into the roadway by a small, slight woman.

Quick reactions enabled him to stop a few feet short of running her over. In the moment of relief and weakness that followed the near accident, he agreed to give her a lift. For the next few minutes she had to listen to him telling her off for leaping out of the hedge. She seemed unconcerned. She was a missionary, she explained. She could rely on God to look after her. She was on her way to speak at a meeting.

The omens for the Taurus were good and the brew, prepared with such care by Philip, proved to be most suitable for toasting the mountains of Turkey. Philip never operated by exact quantities but the drink was made by heating cocoa, honey, spices and black rum. It was his own creation and this was its first moment of truth. We christened it Commedagh Cup. Let the storm do its worst, we were fortified now, both inside and out.

Our few days in the snow were an education and a delight, stolen days in the hills. Later that year and just before we left for the Taurus, I was driving home one evening when I saw what seemed like a familiar figure at the road-side waving for a lift. I knew instantly that this must be the missionary.

I stopped and as we drove, we conversed pleasantly. I introduced the subject of travelling in Asia Minor. She spoke like a pilgrim and we shared our thoughts as if we were old friends. She told me she was to speak at a mission that evening in Newcastle and was to meet the organiser, whose name she had forgotten, at his home, the address of which she had also forgotten. On a previous visit she had visited the house and was sure she would recognise it, when she saw it.

When we reached Newcastle, I drove to the far end. Then, without speaking, I turned into an avenue and stopped at a house.

"But this is the right place," she said "How did you know?"

I felt no need to reply.

"God must have led you here," she said. " He always looks after me wherever I go."

It seemed unnecessary to tell her that I happened to know who was organising the mission. But neither was there any doubt in my mind that God was looking after her.

She had connected us with the Taurus and we had been of some little help to her. Perhaps it was no coincidence, our paths had been meant to cross.

A GHOST KNOCKS ON THE COTTAGE WINDOW

Norman and I knew each other long before we climbed mountains together. We had played rugby for the same team, in the same pack of forwards and there is no better place to learn how a companion will fare when the going is hard. He was a school master by profession and we came together as mountaineers when he involved me in the mountain training of some of his pupils.

The boys were members of the Combined Cadet Corps at a college in Belfast and amongst the keenest aspirant mountaineers I had met. The programme had been known officially in the Corps as Arduous Training but re-designated, Adventure Training, and a professional instructor was required by regulations to be involved.

We trained in the Mournes and Norman organised trips to the Cairngorm Mountains in Scotland. We went in winter and trekked across the great plateau above the ski slopes of Aviemore. Our camp under Ben Macdui, was on a snow covered shelf beside a lake. For shelter we built a great curved wall with blocks of frozen snow, finished, of course, with holes to slow down the wind, as Brian and Philip had taught me in the Mournes. Loch Etchachan was the highest lake in the British Isles and we were told later that it would have been frozen to a depth of three feet when we were there.

There were survival and ice climbing skills to be learned and peaks to be climbed. We melted snow for water and lived on survival rations. At the end of each trip we had a day's skiing which almost seemed a frivolous pursuit after the mountaineering. It was later, and in another country, that I came to see skiing as one of the great mountain skills.

On the second of these expeditions to the Cairngorm we crossed to Glasgow on the night boat. There was an hour's wait before the train was due to leave and Norman went off to see the city. He had been shopping and returned with a carrier bag of food.

"You may find it hard to believe, Bert, but our train has no restaurant car." Norman was clearly not best pleased by this lack of consideration by British Rail but the bag of food was a consolation.

The boys were travelling Second Class but Norman and I had a First Class compartment to ourselves. He was an officer in the Corps and travelled First Class by right. At the beginning of the trip he had presented me with a document which stated that I was 'A Civilian Instructor of Officer Status'. It obviously entitled me to the best seats too. It was a class of travel to which I was not accustomed, but I decided to make the best of it.

The morning slipped by pleasantly as we travelled through the Scottish countryside. At one o'clock Norman rose and pulled the blinds down on the corridor side of the carriage.

"Fancy a spot of lunch?" he said cheerily.

I had been wondering what was in the bag. Norman needed no answer. He spread his newspaper on the seat opposite and laid out the food. There were four eggs, two large lamb chops, a loaf of bread and a small packet of butter.

"You'll need your eating kit," he said and delved in his own rucksac to produce a gas stove, a frying pan, an enamel plate and a knife, fork and spoon set. He set the stove on the floor, lit it and began to fry the chops in butter. I sat back and watched in admiration. The delicious smell of cooking lamb filled the carriage.

"Your lunch will only be a moment, Sir." Norman was turning the chops. "Perhaps you would be kind enough to butter the bread."

The chops were done and Norman was frying the eggs when there was a knock on the door.

I slid it open and a uniformed ticket collector stopped in amazement on the threshold, nostrils twitching in the appetising aroma.

"Good afternoon," said Norman, holding out our tickets. "Hope our chaps are behaving themselves in the second class seats."

The ticket collector's eyes were fixed on the eggs sizzling in the pan. His mouth was open. He appeared to be trying to speak.

"Very poor show there's no restaurant car," said Norman severely. "Fortunately we're able to fend for ourselves."

The ticket collector clipped the tickets without a word. He stepped back quickly and slid the door closed, as if to shut the scene out of his mind. I knew by the look on his face he had already decided that, if questioned by superiors, he had seen nothing out of the ordinary in this carriage.

"Didn't have much to say for himself," said Norman cheerily, "Might at least have wished us 'Bon appetit'. Fancy a second egg?"

The trip had started well.

We spent four days crossing the snow bound Cairngorm, climbing peaks, camping high. For the last two nights of the expedition we pitched our tents beside the frozen Pools of Dee at the highest point in the Lairig Ghru. The Lairig Ghru is one of the great high valleys of the mountains of Scotland. It rises to almost 3,000 feet and cuts through the vast plateau of Cairngorm from north to south, a distance of perhaps thirty miles.

My responsibilities were almost over. The trek had gone well. It was our last day and we had climbed the East Face of Braeriach, one of the highest peaks in the range. It had been an ascent of quality, at the limit of what the boys could be expected to climb on snow and ice.

Within twenty feet of the top we had arrived underneath the lip of a huge overhanging ice cornice and had tunnelled through it to reach the summit. The boys were ecstatic. Norman was delighted.

For a group of seventeen-year-old boys such as this, the challenge has to be pitched at exactly the right level. Too easy and little is learned. It may even encourage a less than respectful attitude to mountains such as these. However if the challenge is pitched too high, the risks increase dramatically. Because of the severity of the winter conditions and the vast scale of the range, a simple accident in this terrain can have the most serious consequences.

Now we were back at the camp I noticed Norman was angry. I had never before seen him so irate. When they arrived at their tents the boys had simply dumped the climbing gear in a heap, ropes, ice axes all thrown down together in the snow. It was not just the moment of carelessness which annoyed him. These were his boys. They had shared a few special days with us. Now he felt that they had let him down at the end of the trip.

He gave me a cup of coffee and I took it across to their tents.

They gathered around expecting to be told off. But it was the wrong time for that.

"I know you intend to sort the gear out before we leave in the morning," I said. "But we may not have finished for the day. We've made it back to camp. Someone else may not be so lucky," I pointed at the steep slopes all around.

"If there's an accident on one of those hills, we'll all want to help. No point in excuses if you're not able to, because your ropes and ice axes are in a tangled frozen mass."

Twenty mimutes later one of the boys came my tent.

"We're sorry about that, Bert," he said.

I grinned at him.

"I knew you wouldn't mind me mentioning it." After the day's climb I reckoned they owed me an audience.

That night we were staying at the Army Ski Hut at Rothiemurchus and after dinner Norman and I went down to a local hotel for a celebratory drink. We were just installed in a nook near the fire when there was a telephone call for me. It was the leader of the local mountain rescue team. He had rung the Ski Hut looking for assistance on a rescue and one of our boys had told him how to find us.

"A climber has been seriously injured in a fall above the Lairig Ghru," he said, "We're leaving now to bring him off the slope. We need a relief party to carry him down the Ghru. Can you raise a group and meet us at the Pools of Dee at midnight?"

Back at the Ski Hut, the personnel staying there disappeared when the rescue party was mentioned. I was approached by a sergeant in a Highland Regiment.

"I have a party of other ranks, sir. They're not here to ski. It's a punishment detail. They've been cleaning up the place. They've all volunteered."

I left at ten with my auxiliary rescue team made up from the punishment detail and as many of our party as were fit to go. We reached the Pools of Dee at midnight and stood on the same spot where we had camped the previous night. The real mountain rescue team lowered the stretcher with the injured climber down the last few feet of the slope.

They were tired. It had been a hard descent in bleak conditions. The patient was badly injured. The team leader supervised the handing over of the stretcher to our care. To my great relief the doctor who had climbed with the team to the site of the accident was to stay with us, to keep checking on the patient.

Ours was an easier task than the first part of the rescue. It was a dark night, it was icy cold and we had to carry the stretcher as smoothly as possible on the steep rocky path down the Lairig Ghru. But there was a track and the young soldiers were fit and willing.

We reached the Ski Hut after four a.m. and saw the patient off to hospital in a Land Rover. I thanked my team members and sat down for a cup with the sergeant in charge of the punishment detail.

"Your lads were great," I said and he smiled.

"There's a few of our officers wouldnay agree with you."

He told me they were in a Highland Regiment, recruited in Glasgow and had just completed a tour of duty in Europe with NATO.

"They gave us a wee bit of trouble when we were in Germany." It was unclear to me whether the trouble was caused by the soldiers or the Germans.

"The locals called us the Poison Dwarfs and we're stuck with it." He and I laughed and shook hands.

When you go back," I said, "Tell those officers that the Poison Dwarfs did a grand job.

At breakfast next morning one of our boys said what the others were thinking.

"If that accident had happened the previous evening, we would have been there, at our camp at the Pools of Dee."

There was no need to discuss what might have been. It was enough for them to realise, that those who go into the mountains need to be able to help each other.

Back home in Northern Ireland a few days later, I telephoned the Scottish mountain rescue team. The accident victim had been a student at a university in Scotland. His head injuries had been very serious and sadly, he had died in hospital two days after his rescue from the hills.

....

Norman was a great man for contacts. Before we left he arranged for us to meet a high ranking RAF officer, who just happened to be skiing in the area. It must have been an Air-vice Marshal or some such exalted personage. As a result, our trip the next year was to Arctic Norway.

There were seven of us in the party, four seventeen-year-old boys, Norman, another master at the school called Alwyn and myself. We flew to Bodo in North Norway in an ancient RAF Shackleton bomber converted to survey Russian shipping movements in the North Sea. The Royal Norwegian Air Force were our hosts in Bodo and provided a sergeant as instructor in ski trekking.

We travelled through the vast Arctic snowscape on the Arctic Railway which connects Bodo with the south of the country. The train made a stop to let us alight at one of the small huts which had been built every ten kilometres along the railway line as emergency shelters.

The huts were small two-storey buildings constructed of two layers of wood with insulation between. They were double glazed and had a pot-bellied wood-burning stove on each floor. The refrigerator was a snow bank outside and inside, with the stoves lit, the huts were warm and comfortable.

We were there in April and Northern Norway had emerged from the depths of a winter when the sun never rises, the time they call 'the long dark tunnel'. The outside temperature at 8 a.m. was usually 42°F or 24°C below freezing and by noon it had risen but was still 22°F or 12°C below.

This is the Nordland region and we were amongst the peaks of the Semskfjell Range. The map showed that the railway line was in a valley but there was no sign of the river. It would have been frozen solid under many feet of snow. No one lived nearby. The valley would be used for summer grazing for the reindeer but now the nearest habitation was a tiny railway station at Stodi, ten miles to the south.

Karl, the Norwegian Air Force sergeant, taught us to trek on skis in this magnificent, empty landscape. All around there were peaks to be climbed but they could only be reached on skis. On foot, our boots would have sunk into the snow, knee deep. We all had a little down-hill skiing experience but this was the real thing.

We clumped up little hills, herring-bone fashion, and slithered down the other side. We learned the rhythm of moving on the flat, the slide forward, the squeeze of the legs, the push to slide again. Soon we could move at jogging speed and could manage to keep the stride going uphill.

On one of these training sessions I stopped to admire the finest of the peaks. It was Semskefj, its skyline a great snow dome. It rose steeply above a small glacier, the rock cliffs of its south face separated by bands of snow and split to one side by a couloir. Without removing my inner gloves, I sketched the shape in my notebook. This could be our peak.

Two days later we trekked up to its base. We removed our skis and stuck them point upwards in the snow, exchanging the smooth surfaces for the steel spikes of crampons which we strapped on in their place.

One of the boys touched the head of his ice axe with his glove off and his skin froze to the metal. His friend told him he had no choice but to rip the hand away and leave the skin on the axe head. I breathed my hot breath to melt the join and wondered who would help the helper, if my lips touched the metal and froze to it too. Would they leave me to tear my lips away?

Norman led one rope, with Alwyn and two of the boys, and the couloir as their route. I led the other with Karl at the lower end of the rope and two boys tied on between us. We were attempting the South Face.

The snow was firm to the base of the rocks and we followed the bands of snow between the cliffs. It was a complicated route, but it was not the difficulty of the climbing that made it hard. The snow was in powder form. It had probably fallen months before, but in the extreme cold it had never compacted into the frozen snow the climber calls ice and which makes for speedy, relatively safe ascents.

In the Alps and Scotland, and in the Mournes too, when there is a good fall of snow, the melting and freezing, as the temperature rises and falls, causes the snow to consolidate. The conditions on Semskefj were unlike any I had ever experienced. We climbed slowly and with great care.

The last 120 feet of the climb was on firm, stable snow, which was just as well, for here the face was at its steepest and most exposed.

We met Norman's party on the top and celebrated our first Arctic summit with squares of chocolate. This was, almost certainly, the first time these routes had been climbed and we were exhilarated. But for me the best was yet to come.

On the way down, Norman and I stopped to look back at the face and check our routes against the little sketch I had made two days before. The best place to observe a mountain is from some distance away. Viewed from underneath, it is hard to see more than the first few feet of a face, unless the slope is gentle. The routes we had chosen from the sketch were the routes that had been climbed.

Karl and the others headed down to the hut. When we started our descent, Norman led and I followed on a different line. Soon he was out of sight and I skied on my own, sweeping down from one little valley to another.

At 5,000 feet, Semskefj was hardly one of the world's high mountains. It was being in this place however, in the midst of a vast snow-bound panorama, which made it such a satisfying climb for all of us. And now there was the descent on skis. But the joy was not in the speed or the excitement of the long run down.

I knew I was not skiing in a style which would have pleased an expert, but well enough to let me descend safely. This was the way to traverse snow-clad terrain. The skis rattled on ridged ice. They swished through the softer snow. The rocks and hillocks seemed to rush by, gathering speed.

I had a feeling of travelling through this Arctic landscape on a mystical course, as if I had been here before, and was retracing my journey.

Three months later, Norman and I were in the mountains again. This time in Turkey, as members of the Ulster Taurus Expedition. From the cold of the Arctic in April, to the heat of Asia Minor in July, it seems now to have been but one short step.

We went back to Turkey three years later, with a second Ulster expedition and shared what we thought then was another first ascent. With Brian, the man from the ministry, and Seamus, one of the younger members, we climbed the East Face of Kaldi Dag. I led one rope with Brian and Norman led the other with Seamus.

It was a rock climb of epic length and, unprepared except for emergency bivouac sheets, we had to sleep the night on the mountain. Our only sustenance that evening was a bar of survival rations which none of us could eat raw. Then Seamus discovered two boiled sweets in a pocket. It mattered not that they were fluff covered. They were divided in two with ceremony and we each savoured our morsel.

Back in Ireland Norman and I continued to climb together. One evening, after a good day on the slabs of Slieve Bernagh, we stayed the night at a little cottage on the open mountainside. We had the place to ourselves. It was older than Castelgandolfo, probably built in Georgian times by the noble lord who owned the estate, for one of his tenants.

It had a fine arched doorway and was perched above the forest. The view was across the County Down countryside, to Slieve Croob and beyond to the Black Mountain on the other side of Belfast.

After dinner we sat by the open fire and drank a glass of red wine, talking of peaks and mountain journeys, of Arctic snow and Turkish yoghurt, and of the next expedition, this time to Afghanistan.

I slept on an upper bunk on one side of the room and Norman took the narrow bed at the other side of the fire.

At the darkest hour of the night I was wakened by a knock on the window. Someone was tapping on the pane with their knuckles.

"Nap-nap... NAP! NAP! NAP!... Nap-nap-nap-nap."

I heard Norman stirring. We both knew the cottage's secret.

Years ago a middle-aged couple had lived here. The small-holding was a good living and they were happy. There was, of course, a hornet in their paradise. From time to time the husband would take himself off to the pub for a drinking bout.

When he returned, the quiet, loving man became a violent bully. He threw his meal in the fire. He shouted abuse at his wife. He beat her and sometimes threw her out onto the cobbled 'street', as it was called, in front of the cottage.

After an hour or two, he would let her back into the house and in the morning, her own misery would melt away as she comforted him in the depths of his remorse.

One winter's night he returned drunk, but in an even greater rage than usual. He punched his wife. He threw her outside and locked the door. He dropped into his favourite chair by the fire and fell asleep.

His wife banged on the door but he snored on in a drunken slumber. It began to snow and she felt weaker. For hours she knocked on the door and the window but he lay sprawled in his chair by the fire.

She slumped down on the doorstep, trying to shelter from the snow, waiting for morning. The light wakened her husband. He rose and called for his wife to make him something to eat. Save for himself, the house was empty. He opened the door and there she was, lying dead on the doorstep.

As long as he lived, he was wakened at night by someone knocking to get in. He shook with fear but never rose from his bed. He knew that to open the door would have been to face the ghost of a loving wife, ill-used, and dead by his hand.

"Nap-nap-nap-nap… Nap-nap-nap-nap-nap-nap!"

The knocking was more urgent now.

I sat up on one elbow and found my torch to look at my watch. It was 4 a.m. I knew that Norman was awake. He was lying still, trying to pretend he was asleep but he was too still. Norman was not a noisy sleeper but never as quiet as this.

"NAP!… NAP!… NAP!… NAP-NAP-NAP-NAP!"

It was louder than ever.

"Bert, I think someone may be trying to gain entrance." Norman's tone indicated that he was not the one who should rise.

"All right," I said heroically. "I'll go." If it was the ghost of the wife, I had no intention of being in bed when she entered the cottage.

I slid down from the bunk and into my boots and unbolted the front door. There was no one outside. It was not yet time for the first light of dawn, but as often happens in the mountains at night, there was enough light to see the immediate surroundings. I looked down the street between the cottage and the wall and around the back. There was no one there and nowhere for anyone to hide.

I came back inside and bolted the door. As I climbed back up to my bunk, the knocking started again.

"Nap-nap-nap-nap… nap… nap… nap."

Now it was more feeble.

This time I knew it had to be the ghost of times past. I slid down from the bunk and, barefooted, opened the door. There was no one outside. I looked around the sides but there was no sign of human or beast. As I came back to the door, my eye caught a flicker in the window. Inside, I drew back the curtain and found our ghost.

It was a jackdaw trapped between window pane and curtain, knocking with the bony joint of its wing against the glass.

"Nap-nap-nap… nap-nap-nap."

The jackdaw must have entered the cottage by falling down the chimney during the night. It found itself trapped inside, as the wife had been trapped outside. The bird's survival required our help to be let out, as the woman required her husband's help to be let in.

Norman rose and between us we shooed the jackdaw to the open door. As it streaked off into the night sky, I fancied it looked back as it squawked its thanks.

They say every apparently supernatural happening has a scientific or natural explanation but there are those, like the Buddhist, who believe in the reincarnation of the spirit after death.

Call it a ghost, or a flight of fancy if you will, but for me, the spirit of that long dead woman was in the jackdaw.

And I have never felt better than I did that night when we released her to the freedom of the hills.

FOLLOW THE ULSTER WAY

It was nine o'clock in the morning, in the Soho Car Park in the town of Newry. The air was cool and damp. It was doing its best to rain. Straggles of mist lay on the backs of the Carlingford mountains. As we had driven over the Mournes from Newcastle earlier, the higher peaks had been hidden by snatches of cloud, like wisps of dirty sheep's wool caught on a whin bush.

Unreasonable people may have considered that it was not much of a day for the end of summer. They could be as dissatisfied as they liked, Teddy and I were pleased with the weather. It could be a lot worse, we reasoned. It would do as it was, a grand day for what we had in front of us.

Soho Car Park is beside the Newry Canal and in the centre of the town. There were a few cars but the lack of people bothered us. We had been promised a crowd but the place was empty. Had we come on the wrong day? Had we made a mistake about the time?

Sport for All Week, organised by the Sports Council, was due to begin in two days time and Teddy and I had agreed, as our contribution, to spend nine days walking sections of the Ulster Way. Uncharitable colleagues may have felt that we had 'volunteered' for the walk, just to get away from the bedlam of mass participation schemes, awareness campaigns, rallies, competitions and a 'Special Event' featuring a Government Minister canoeing on the River Lagan. Later we were sorry to have missed this last-named treat. The Rt. Hon. Gentleman made it 'Special' by capsizing in the less-than-inviting waters of the Lagan.

Our trek was meant to encourage walking on newly opened sections of the Ulster Way and an open invitation had been issued to anyone who would like to accompany us on any of the nine stages. Our daily starting points and times had been announced on radio and in the press. We had been told to expect a large number on the first day to give us a good start, but thereafter we would have to cope with whoever turned up.

Our journey around the Province was also meant to publicise walking as a healthy form of exercise and to encourage local authorities to waymark routes. We had no intentions, however, of allowing such duties to spoil a nine-day journey through some of the best countryside in Western Europe.

The idea of a long-distance walking route around the Province, like the Pennine Way in Britain, was not new. The idea had been proposed in the forties but had not been officially approved until 1974, three years previously. Only a few sign posts had, as yet, been erected, but the planned line of the entire route existed on a map, and we had a copy.

Wilfrid Capper, the man who inspired the Ulster Way was the first to appear. Wilfrid had, of course, been involved in the original proposal for the route, as he had been in virtually every positive move for the previous forty years, to preserve the Ulster countryside or improve our opportunities to enjoy it.

Wilfrid was here to see us off and to make sure we found the way, at least on the first section.

"Where's the great horde of people you were promised?" he said, not really expecting either of us to answer, especially at this hour and on a damp morning.

As we talked to him about the route, the Soho Car Park began to fill up. Soon it was packed with cars, mini-buses and people. The vehicles were parked anywhere the driver could find a space. The people milled around, waving to friends, chatting, shouting greetings. As colourful and animated a mob as I had ever met.

It might not be a fine day but this was a happy crowd. Were they here to see us off?

There were scores of young people, many of whom had arrived by mini-bus and were in school uniform, as if straight from school, after morning assembly. There were mothers with children by the hand. I counted four press photographers, two priests and five policemen in uniform, trying to shift the people, to let the drivers park their cars.

A group of local politicians, led by the Chairman of Newry and Mourne Council, appeared on foot. Did this mean they intended to join the walk? Raymond, the council's Recreation and Tourism Officer, was with them. He smiled the smile of a contented man. It would have been his job to organise the official send off and this enthusiastic throng was his reward.

A party of well equipped mountaineers from the mountaineering club of a local girls' grammar school had obviously been told to act as marshals. A crowd of young people buzzed around them like a swarm of bees, demanding Sport For All stickers. The marshals were rounding them up, like bouncers outside a disco.

Adult walkers arrived by car in twos and threes and stared in amazement at the horde, before reluctantly putting on their anoraks and boots.

"Are they here to see us off?" one of them asked nervously, hoping that this was indeed the case.

"No way," said Teddy with his customary consideration for the intrepid, "They're all going with us." The walkers paled.

For once in our lives Teddy and I stood back, nonplussed. The pair of us had led walking and mountaineering groups for years. He was warden of Tollymore, the Northern Ireland Mountain Centre and leader of the Mourne Mountain Rescue Team. We had just returned from a mountaineering expedition to Iran which I had led. But here in our own country, faced with this huge mob, we had no idea how to get started.

"There must be hundreds of them, Bert. How do..." His voice trailed away. Teddy was lost for words. Help, however, was at hand.

The Chairman of the Council and his party came over. John McAvoy was a tall and amiable man whose council's area included part of counties Down and Armagh. I had admired his skill as a council chairman in this part of Ulster for years.

Raymond, the Recreation and Tourism officer, was obviously well used to situations like this. He had a loud voice and a commanding presence. He called for silence. Amazingly, and almost immediately, the roar of the crowd's conversation was stilled.

The Chairman's speech was short and witty. He presented Teddy and me with corn plasters, foot powder and a cooling footspray. The press photographers, led by the man from the Newry Reporter, arranged the three of us, the Chairman in the middle, holding the gifts, like an advertisement for Dr Scholl's Foot Treatments. The crowd cheered.

The Chairman shook hands with us and raised his arm, his fist clenched, with one finger pointing skywards like a starter's pistol. He announced the start of the walk as if it was the opening of a new stretch of motorway. The crowd set off at speed, like the start of a people's marathon. They were leaderless, but determined to make a mark on this early stage.

As the multitude streamed out of the Soho Car Park I shouted to Teddy and Wilfrid,

"You two take the front! And I'll act as sweeper at the back." At a time like this, it requires speedy thinking and a little low cunning to wrest the best job from the likes of Teddy and Wilfrid.

The pair of them shot off like frightened rabbits, scuttling along the outside of the crowd, now in a great crocodile three or four deep. In his youth Wilfrid had been a long-distance runner and was holding his form well. Teddy was a mountain runner, some would say, even when he was meant to be a mountain walker. He was acknowledged by all, except himself, as one of the fittest men in the country. I knew they would make it.

They reached the front and slowed the pace. Teddy making it clear that anyone who passed him would do so at their peril. Wilfrid shouting like a sergeant major leading his troops on a route march, to keep them off the roadway and on the pavement.

Two of the council members were walking this stage and they were well away too, holding prominent places near the front. No local politician dare be left straggling along at the back on a day like this. I thanked the Chairman and the others in his party. Their support was important and they were impressed by the huge numbers of local people who had turned up for the walk. The omens were good for both of the official aims of our walk.

"We appreciate your choice of Newry as a starting point," the Chairman said seriously, "We won't forget it.".

I knew what he meant. With one large city in a relatively small province, big events tended to be launched in Belfast. Media coverage was virtually assured, as was interest in taking part. But Newry had been an obvious choice for the start of the walk. The Ulster Way went through its streets, we knew of the great enthusiasm there for the outdoors and anyway, it was one of my favourite towns.

I hurried off and caught up with a priest who, as befits his calling was showing a sense of responsibility, and had taken up duty at the rear of the party. He and I both knew that, in the Holy Land, the shepherd led his flocks from the back. I settled in beside him, looking forward to his conversation.

Ahead the police had stopped the traffic on the main Belfast to Dublin road through the town, to let our caravan pass without hindrance.

As I crossed the road the RUC sergeant leaned towards me.

"Three hundred and sixty-two or there abouts," he said with a wink. "Just in case you want to check that you haven't lost any by the time you reach Rostrevor."

A long way ahead at the front of the column, and at the crest of a hill, Teddy turned and gave me a wave. I knew what he meant. All was well at the head of this horde. But I knew too, that it was a gesture of jubilation. We were on our way.

Our route followed a quiet country road and the weather brightened as we climbed above the coast. There were patches of sparkling water on Carlingford Lough as the sun found holes in the cloud. On the other side of the lough, the long ridge on the Cooley peninsula, from the Carlingford Mountain to the Raven's Rocks, was swept clear of mist. One day, I hoped, there might be a path across those hills to link up with the Ulster Way at Newry.

"Isn't it just great to see them all here," said the priest. "She didn't intend to come, you know." He pointed ahead at a woman in a long raincoat, carrying a shopping bag.

"She was leaving the children to the start and she couldn't resist joining in. That'll be the lunch in the bag." Like any good man of the cloth, he not only knew what his flock were up to, but why they were up to it.

We by-passed Warrenpoint and reached Rostrevor in the sunshine. This was the end of the stage as far as most of the walkers were concerned, but not for us. They piled into buses and mini-buses to be ferried back to Newry and we met Raymond for a meal at a local hotel.

It was a long stop and late in the afternoon when we left for the next part of the stage. Raymond was checking the dates of our schedule.

"I'll see you at the finish," he said cryptically. It could not mean that he would be seeing us at the end of that day, for we were due to camp in the mountains. It was the end of the ninth day before we discovered what he meant.

Our route now took us across the Western Mournes. Only the hardiest of the walkers intended to do this section. The way now lies through the forest as far as Leitrim Lodge and then on a good track to Pierce's Castle, but Wilfrid had asked us to try a route through the mountains. It led across the Red Bog of Kilbroney and the hill of Thievedockdarragh.

In good conditions it is a fine mountain walk, but the evening closed in and it was a very tired and hungry party that made it to Pierce's Castle at 9:30 p.m., having covered the last few miles in the dark.

Pierce's Castle is a rocky summit below Eagle Mountain. The camping detail, led by our friend Sr. Mark, was already there, mini-bus parked on the track a few hundred yards away.

Teddy and I left at nine the next morning on Day Two while the others cleared up and struck camp. We had miles to go across the mountain and another group to meet.

They were waiting for us on the Brandy Pad, where the Hare's Gap acts as the gateway to the Eastern Mournes. There were perhaps two dozen walkers from YHANI, the youth hostel association, two students, a dog and a two-year old baby. We also found that Jim, a youth worker friend, was still with us having started in Newry and spent the night at the Pierce's Castle camp.

"What kept ye?" one of the bolder ones asked, not meaning to be cheeky, but risking it all the same.

Had the same cheery greeting met us three or four days later on the walk, when the going was hard, the reply might have been different.

"We've half-a-day's walking behind us," said Teddy. "I suppose you've just waddled up the Trassey Track."

They were a light-hearted crowd. Their wit and banter took no prisoners. Their good spirits were infectious. I had been wondering whether the people who came to walk with us each day would be a help or a hindrance. If the first two days were anything to go by, we were going to enjoy the company.

Some of the girls from the school mountaineering club also arrived to join us. I had thought that yesterday would have been far enough but clearly, they would not be easily shaken off.

I now discovered that two of them had volunteered to travel with us on the whole journey. They would keep in contact with the Sports Council, report our progress to the press and radio stations, buy food, check on the accommodation. It was a job which required initiative. We had no such luxury as a support vehicle. In order to make their telephone contacts and arrive at the accommodation before us, they would have to seek lifts from those who came to visit and sometimes trust to hitch-hiking.

Deirdre and Yvonne were about fifteen or sixteen years of age, optimistic, dynamic, given to practical jokes and banter, unruly and amazingly reliable. They took to the job as if they had been specially chosen and had been in training for years. Their reward would be, if indeed reward it was, to walk with us for at least part of each day's stage.

They had their own ways of working. No task was too difficult, as long as we were not aware of how it was accomplished. By the end of the trip they seemed to know everyone, press and radio contacts, Sports Council personnel, youth hostel wardens, staff at the outdoor centres we visited, local dignitaries and the hundreds of walkers who joined us.

Teddy and I never knew where they were, who they were speaking to in the media or what they were up to, unless we had them with us on the walk. At times we wondered if Sr. Mark had landed us with these two to pay us back for some unremembered slight.

It was encouraging to meet such enthusiasm from the walkers who had taken the trouble to come for the day's walk. I was not surprised to see YHANI so well represented. The association had been formed originally by walkers and cyclists and I had been a member for years. Not surprisingly of course, it was an organisation of which Wilfrid Capper had been one of the founders.

The happy throng rambled across the Brandy Pad, new friends and old. We reached the shoulder of Slieve Beg, about half way to Newcastle and I saw Teddy, who was at the front of the group, look up to his left towards Slieve Corragh. He turned and jerked his head in the direction of the ridge. I knew what he was thinking.

Two years before he and I had been involved in a night search in this area. A group of young people had failed to turn up at a rendez-vous the previous afternoon and their leaders had become concerned for their safety. Teddy was the rescue team leader and we had searched for hours in the dark. It was a windy night, with mist and heavy showers of rain. At 3:30 a.m. it seemed time to call off the search until daylight. As the others left for base, Teddy and I decided to make one last sortie.

We left the Brandy Pad and followed a compass bearing to the ridge of Slieve Corragh. At the top, the Mourne Wall loomed out of the darkness. We looked over and the mist swirled up from the Pot of Legawherry, the edge of the cliff only a few yards from the wall. In a few seconds we had scaled the wall and on the ledge between its base and the edge of the sheer cliff were two tiny tents.

I called out a greeting and the tent doors were unzipped. Young heads appeared in the openings. Having lost their bearings in the mist the previous day, they had decided, as we had guessed, to make for the Mourne Wall. Once over the wall, there was shelter from the wind but their way down was blocked by the cliffs. Sensibly they had pitched camp on the ledge to wait for morning.

They would have managed without our help but it was a relief to us and to their leaders, to have found them safe and well and in good form. We showed the boys their position on the map and left them where they were until daylight.

I gave Teddy a wave at the head of our crowd. The Ulster Way Walk was well underway.

We reached Newcastle in great good humour and the party dispersed for the cafes and ice cream parlours and, who knows, maybe even the pubs. Sr. Mark and the girls were staying at the Tollymore Centre and they left too, but Teddy and I were not finished. Our day was due to end at Dundrum.

The tide was out and we walked the empty three-mile beach on our own. Near the bar mouth which leads to Inner Dundrum Bay, we stopped and turned to look back. The Mournes were miles away, a little group of peaks on a far horizon.

I had a strange sense that the walk of the past two days only existed as part of a much, much longer journey. A journey far further than this nine-day trek would take us. It is a feeling which returned each time I looked back at a range of hills, on the longer walks I followed later in Spain and Portugal. It seems that each stretch is but a part of a greater odyssey.

The sand became soft near the inner bay and it was good to reach the track through the Murlough Nature Reserve. We had started on Day One with hundreds of companions and finishing by ourselves at Dundrum on Day Two was the natural balance which would keep us on the way.

We met Wilfrid again the next morning at Ballyboley Forest, near Ballyclare in the south of County Antrim. He knew that I had never walked the first part of this section of the Ulster Way before and wanted to be there when we did it. He knew too, that one of the farmers along the route disliked walkers and was reputed to be taking the law into his own hands armed with a shotgun.

There were forty with us when we started, Girl Guides, Ranger Guides, a school group and assorted walkers. Others joined us on the way, including about thirty-five youth hostellers at the standing stone beyond Agnew's Hill. At one stage there were ninety-five of us in a great straggling column, winding our way across the hills.

It proved to be a fine stretch of the Ulster way. On the top of the escarpment at Agnew's Hill there were wonderful views, east across Larne Lough to the Island Magee Peninsula, further north were the tiny islands of the Maidens. Across the North Channel lay the coast of Scotland, pale and hazy in the distance.

I looked for Wilfrid to tell him but he was scouting ahead. If that farmer appeared with his shotgun, Wilfrid would be there to draw his fire. The farmer would have to take care of him before he could tackle the rest of us. We need have no worries for our safety.

We walked the crest of the Sallagh Braes, the great curving cliffs above Carncastle and followed an ancient green road, worn into the hillside to the ridge of Scawt Hill. The famous Coast Road was below us and it was easy to see now why Wilfrid had planned the Ulster Way to follow the coastal ridges rather than the coast. Here we were traffic free, with views beyond the county, to Donegal and Down and beyond the country itself to the Mull of Kintyre.

That night we stayed in Moneyvart Youth Hostel. To the County Down tuned ear, the County Antrim 'v' must have sounded like an 'f'. Yvonne and Deirdre insisted on calling the hostel 'Moneyfart' and neither Teddy nor I had the heart to tell them that it was called 'Money vart'.

On the morning of Day Four I discovered that Jim was still with us. He had come for a couple of days but decided to stay for a few more. He was a quiet man, large, amiable, prone to sudden bursts of fun. We found him a great support.

On day four I discovered Jim was still with us

Catherine was there too. She had been one of the leaders of the Guides and Rangers on the previous day. A quick trip home had allowed her to fetch a few things and now she announced her intention of keeping us company for two more days.

A group from a secondary school were due to meet us at Cushendall. We delayed the start as long as we could and as we prepared to leave, their bus drew up. The teacher-in-charge was embarrassed to be late and angry at the behaviour of some of his pupils on the bus. He had already decided to make them all suffer, innocent or guilty.

"If you don't mind," he said, anxious not to involve us in his problems, "We'll leave you to make your own way for the first stretch. I want to run the steam out of this lot up the big hill out of Cushendun."

They moved off briskly and when we left the main road to Ballycastle to follow the old coach road, they were four or five hundred feet above us, on the steepest way up the hillside. It was the last we saw of them.

The old coach road was a revelation. It cut across the flank of the mountain, two hundred feet or so above the motor road. Below us was Loughareema, or Loughaveema, as it is on some maps, the famous vanishing lake.

This was the way Stanley and I had cycled when we were teenagers on the journey I had called, Beyond the Black Mountain.

We crossed a fine stone bridge on the coach road, still in good repair, a single arch spanning a stream. The route took us to the cliffs of Fair Head and we rambled, at our leisure, past the little lakes and through the rocks at the edge.

Below the precipice at our feet, was the boulder beach and the sea. Five miles away, across the turbulent water of the sound, was the island of Rathlin, like another country beyond the waves. I could never remember a better day's walking in Ireland.

We stayed in comfort at another youth hostel, this time in Ballycastle. Deirdre and Yvonne had hitch-hiked here earlier and bought food for the evening meal. Later I stretched out in my bunk and slowly bent my right foot upwards towards my shin. The achilles tendon at the heel throbbed in pain. I felt a bubbling sensation as the tendon moved in its sheath. It was the classic sign of a damaged achilles. All day the pain had nagged at me. Now I wondered how much further it would let me walk.

Teddy's feet were suffering too, in a new pair of boots. In the morning we changed our footwear. I wore my spare boots which had a slightly higher heel and he took the pair I had been using. They were light and comfortable but the heel had been just too low for me.

Day Five felt longer than it was because we had to wait again for groups, but my tendon and Teddy's feet were on the mend. We were not critical of the groups coming late. They had their own arrangements to fulfil and we were pleased they took the trouble to come to support us.

It is a stunning walk along beach and cliff top from Ballintoy to Portrush. We rounded White Park Bay where Stanley and I had camped on our cycling trip. Benbane Head led to the cliff paths above the Giant's Causeway and there we met our friends from the Runkerry Centre. They had almost given up waiting for us.

For many years Stradreagh in County Derry had been one of my favourite youth hostels. It was small, cosy, like staying in a friend's country cottage, specially vacated by them for the night.

At the beginning and end of every day we had been ferried to starting point or base. Sports Council staff Anne, Dick, Danny and Sally and expedition friends Sam, Frances and Dion had lifted and laid us, some on more than one occasion. The following morning Danny drove us to Castlerock and we walked the Bishop's Road to the escarpment of Binevenagh, with a view across Lough Foyle to the hills of Donegal.

We stopped for lunch in the sunshine and Yvonne complained that she was being eaten alive by the 'midgets'. It was in the days before political correctness, so no one need convince her that the vertically challenged people of County Derry were not attacking her. Rosie had now appeared for the third time, I suspected as much to join Deirdre and Yvonne in their antics, as to walk.

The second night at Stradreagh Hostel was as good as the first. Yvonne and Deirdre were now expert food foragers. If the shop was too far away, they tried the farms. That evening they had bought eggs, tomatoes and grapes from the hostel warden. They swore the man had called them 'grips' and refused to refer to grapes thereafter by any other name.

Teddy and I knew that Day Seven would be long and hard. I had breakfast ready at 7 a.m. It was the best way to get the others up. None of them could resist the smell of bacon, eggs and tomatoes sizzling in a pan.

At Moneyheaney we met yet another school group and they led us on a circular walk over the nearby hill of Crockbrack. It was not part of the Ulster Way but they needed to finish back at their transport.

The detour meant that it was lunch time before we started on the main walk along the ridge to the south of the Glenelly Valley. Across the valley on the north side, the main peaks of the Sperrins were set against a dark sky. The rain threatened but never came.

Before we left, a friend had expressed surprise that I had invited Teddy as my walking companion.

"A nine-day walk with the Hawkins!" he had said, "You pick some strange companions, but this one's like a March hare on the mountain. He'll run you off your feet."

"Don't worry," I had replied, "Teddy's going to enjoy this walk so much he'll forget about running."

I could understand our friend's concern. Teddy was not one to show much sympathy for ill-prepared companions. Aspirant mountain leaders presenting themselves for assessment and allocated him as an assessor, had been known to seek deferment, in order to prepare even more thoroughly or to find some other form of outdoor activity.

Teddy and I had met when he came to an evening fitness class for men which I was taking in Castlewellan some years before. I had been amazed to find the gym full on the first night and said as much to Teddy when he gave me a lift home.

There was an easy explanation.

"At Mass last Sunday," he said, "The priest mentioned the class in the announcements. He made it clear that those who missed such a great opportunity, would have him to answer to."

I knew the Latin for 'a healthy mind, in a healthy body' but this was a new one — 'a healthy spirit, in a healthy body'. It was an interesting approach and good to have a man of the cloth on my side.

So far on the walk Teddy had been the ideal partner, hardy, resourceful, appreciative of everyone who came to walk with us and the most interesting of companions.

But on this day we had need of each other. The detour and the late start had left us well over twenty miles to do across the hills before night. The others who were walking with us turned back to their transport during the afternoon and we kept on at a steady pace. In the early evening we reached a road at the Barnes Gap and just one more hill to climb. Craignamaddy is not high by any standards but I felt the tiredness of the whole eight days looking up at it.

Teddy – The Most Happy of Companions

"I don't know about you," I said, "But I'm getting it tight."

"Me too," said Teddy, with feeling.

The worst that can happen, at a time like this, or on the crux of a climb, is that the partner tries to boost his own flagging energy or nerve by diminishing yours. Teddy's reply was just what I needed. If he was tired too, then it surely was not without cause.

We took Craignamaddy in our stride, chatted the miles away and strolled down into Gortin and to the hostel there at 8:30 p.m. It had been a long day.

Gortin Youth Hostel had once been an RUC barracks, purpose built to withstand bullet and bomb. Its walls were thick, its windows high and small. The dorms had once been cells. But it was comfortable and we had the place to ourselves.

The girls had foraged for food and bought us a few beers as a special treat. They had noticed that our appetites had increased as the days passed and made us a huge meal. They were doing well, almost well enough to earn a compliment.

That evening they began to disclose some of the true stories of their escapades. At Moneyvart they had climbed on to the roof of the hostel for some reason that even Teddy's close questioning could not uncover. It seemed to have something to do with a man who had lost a hand and who insisted on showing them the various gadgets he could screw on in its place. The escapade was later verified by a photograph of Yvonne posing on the hostel roof.

In North Antrim they had been given a lift by a 'creepy' man. A newspaper reporter who was drunk, had grabbed Deirdre's arm and taken them into a cafe for coffee. I pitied the 'creepy' man and the drunk. Had either tried anything on with this pair, he would surely not have lived to regret it.

In North Derry they had pinched apples from an orchard and outrun the chasing farmer. They had chatted up Australian hostellers. Yvonne gave us evidence too, of the power of prayer. Having failed to get a lift at a time when one was needed urgently, she blessed herself and stuck out her thumb. A Land Rover stopped immediately and the driver went out of his way to take them to their destination.

They had found a Sport For All sticker in the loo at the Giant's Causeway, been interviewed by the press and radio, walked miles every day, fallen into a bog hole, helped the faint and weary, even cooked a few meals and washed an odd dish.

Photographs later showed that they always posed alluringly with their mouths open, like film stars of the sixties.

It was a long drive to the start of Day Eight in a forest, south of Lower Lough Erne. Fermanagh and Moyle District Councils had been the first two councils to open sections of the Ulster Way and here we were due to walk Fermanagh's Navar and Big Dog Trails from the Lough Navar View Point to Belcoo.

Teddy and I started on our own and crossed the low hills on narrow paths through forest, past tiny lakes set in open bog or hidden in dells. An ancient drove road led over a ridge, its surface churned to mud by the cattle. We laughed, remembering a walker complaining about the state of this section. Did he not know that this track had been used by cattle since the days when men walked only because they had to?

Little Dog and Big Dog were small shapely hills set in finest walking terrain. The paths took us through bog and forest rising to viewpoints where

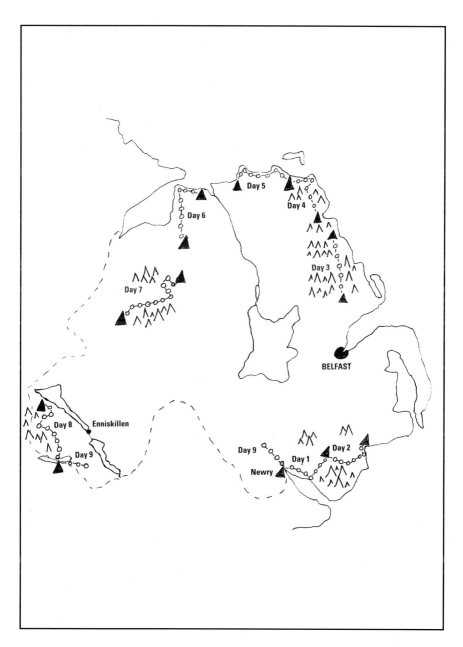

The nine-day Ulster Way Walk

the whole of Fermanagh was laid out before us. Every few yards there was a new prospect. In places this was like the most interesting of Irish mountain terrain, but in miniature.

We had now walked in five of Northern Ireland's six counties and every day the land was different. It felt like moving from country to country rather than county to county.

The rain began to fall, softly, steadily. We reached a road and saw a large plastic sheet in the shape of a mound on the verge. It was sheltering the only two visiting walkers to join us that day. Antony and Dick were eminent members of the legal profession. Dick had been in Iran with us and Antony was later to climb my favourite peak in the Pyrenees with me.

With minds honed razor sharp by their trade they had reasoned that this was the day on which we had least likelihood of company, but being the penultimate walk, the one on which we would have most need of companions.

They rose from beneath the plastic sheet, like tinkers who have eventually, though reluctantly, decided to leave their shelter under the hedge and face the rain. The sight raised our spirits to the very end of the day. As of course, did their company.

Nearby, under the same hedge, was a plastic bivouac bag and packed into it the faithful Deirdre and Yvonne, trying bravely to rouse themselves from a deep sleep, determined to finish the walk with us.

They packed up and the six of us walked on in the rain to Blacklion. We crossed the border into Belcoo and back into Northern Ireland a short distance further, when we reached Gortatole Outdoor Education Centre on the shore of Lower Lough Macnean.

The centre was officially closed but Raymond, the Director, was a friend of many mountain days. He had in his absence left us the run of the place and the hospitality of a well stocked fridge.

We showered, for the first time since we had left the Mournes, played table tennis and pool and even switched on the TV for a few seconds. For dinner we grilled steak with sweet corn, peas and potatoes and drank the red wine of the Spanish Pyrenees. This was followed by a huge fresh cream cake, coffee and biscuits.

At dinner Deirdre and Yvonne were presented with special Sport For All plaques. The Plaques had never been so hard earned or more richly deserved. The girls were almost overcome.

It was still raining in the morning when a group of mainly young people came to walk with us to Florence Court. It rained down on our little party more heavily by the mile. Beautiful Florence Court was hung with wisps of watery mist and we parted with the local people at its gates, grateful that they had still come on such a day.

We travelled slowly by car towards Jerrettspass, due to reach there by mid-afternoon for the last leg of the walk into Newry. We crossed Lady Craigavon Bridge across Upper Lough Erne, then drove through County Tyrone and into County Armagh. Bandit Country the media had taken to calling these parts. It just looked wet to us, as if all the villages and farms had closed down for the day.

At Jerrettspass it was still raining and groups of young people were gathering to walk with us on the final stretch into Newry. There were at least six parties from schools, some from more than twenty miles away. There was a detachment from a Church Lads Brigade company in Craigavon, Guides and Scouts, Catholic Scouts, Youth Club members.

They were mainly young people but there were adults too, and some hardy parents had brought their equally hardy children. There were capes and umbrellas, plastic macs, aroraks, sou'westers, Wellington boots, shoes, walking boots, trainers, plastic bags with holes for arms and legs. Everyone seemed in great good humour. It was as if the bad weather had raised the spirits because we were all out in it, under the same deluge.

Someone gave a signal and the cavalcade started on its way. We had thought of following the canal but not on this evening, not with this crowd, not in these conditions.

In a country with a reputation for marches, this was one parade that could raise no one's ire. Had there been spectators, they might have laughed at the cut of us, but no one could point the finger of anger. My heart went out to the teachers and youth leaders who had organised these groups, to the parents who had brought their children, to the adults and young people who had come to brave the worst of Ulster weather in support of us and our cause.

Many of them had started out with us on Day One and it was as if they had been with us in spirit, every step of the way.

As we neared Newry a car appeared out of the gloom. It was Raymond, the council's chief recreation and tourism officer. He jumped out of his car and stopped the march.

"You'll have to wait for a few minutes. The band is late. They're bound to show up any minute." He was delighted to see us but I detected a note of concern in his voice.

"Band!" said Teddy to me with his first worried look of the whole walk. "What band? If any of the mountaineering crowd see us we're finished. We'll never hear the end of it."

"It's the price of fame," I said cheerfully, hoping that the band had refused to turn out on such a bad evening.

But the band must have feared Raymond more than the weather. Their mini-bus appeared and he had them marshalled and ready to move in minutes.

He gave the command and the march began, led by a grand Irish Pipe band. To give them their due they were playing at full roar, drums enclosed in plastic bags, saffron kilts already dripping on the bare knees.

I saw Teddy look me up and down.

"Only you and I could get away with it," he said.

I could see what he meant. He was dressed from head to ankle in green, green waterproof jacket, green overtrousers, only my brown boots that he had borrowed, peeped out below the trousers. I was wearing my usual white socks, knee length, pulled up over blue overtrousers, topped with a bright red anorak.

Maybe he was right. The mountain centre at Tollymore, twenty miles away, where Teddy was warden and once I had worked, had been blown up a few years before by a terrorist bomb. No one had been hurt but the wave of support from the whole community had carried us on to a bigger and better building on the same site and far greater opportunities for its work.

The morning after the explosion, Teddy and I had stood amongst the wreckage looking at the huge hole in the roof.

"It's nice to have somewhere to come back to," I said by way of consolation, "But we're very fortunate that mountaineering takes place in the mountains." Teddy had laughed and resumed courses a few days later with a plastic sheet over the hole in the roof.

The procession wound its way through Newry to the Soho Car Park. Had anyone wished to know why this town had been chosen as the start and finish of our Ulster Way walk, all they needed to do was to join us and our friends here at its end.

John, the Chairman of the Council was waiting with a phalanx of his most doughty councillors. They sheltered under massive golf umbrellas, the rain cascading from this forest of canopies, splashing on the ground.

His speech was the shortest ever recorded by any council chairman or mayor in the history of the Province. He was impressed by the throng of walkers and in a few words, he did them justice. They deserved it. The walk had been undertaken for them and the reward for Teddy and me was that they had taken part, that they had come in their droves on the good days and even on this rain soaked evening.

It was a walk that neither of us would forget. The countryside of Ulster, taken at this pace, makes its own impression. The local people that we met, whose different accents might at times have been different languages, welcomed us with kindness and hospitality. And those who walked with us had cheered us almost every step of the way.

POSTSCRIPT
A few weeks later Newry and Mourne District Council held a presentation at the Town Hall. The place was packed and there was a certificate for hundreds of local walkers who had taken part, with the grateful thanks of the District Council and us all.

IN THE FOOTSTEPS OF THE PEDLAR POET
OF EXMOOR

At the age of fourteen, in the year 1899, my father left North Devon to become a jockey. It must have been a wrench for a boy who loved the countryside and the moors and his home on a farm called Hunnawins, between Exmoor and the River Bray. He grew up with horses on the farm and ponies on the Moor but, although he worked with horses and rode them all his life, he never realized his young ambition. In those days professional jockeys had to weigh less than nine stone and he became the next best thing, a stud groom.

He came to Belfast a few years before World War 1 with a consignment of brood mares, was offered a job at stables on the outskirts of the city, and made Northern Ireland his second home. On a good day he would say that he stayed because Ulster was the best place he had ever seen. On a bad day it was a different story. The crossing on the cattle boat from Liverpool had been so rough, he had decided that living in Northern Ireland would be preferable to facing the Irish Sea again.

I was born when he was forty-three and in later life he still retained his Devonshire accent although he had left the county fifty years before. He called a 'recipe', a 'receipt' and I still feel embarrassed at the times I tried to correct him. It was only years later that I learned that in times past, 'receipt' was the word used for what is called now a 'recipe'.

He had his own 'receipts' and felt that no man deserved to eat well unless he could cook as well as he could eat. He could make apple tarts and apple dumplings but missed the Devon cream and cider to accompany them. At Hunnawins, when the apples were picked and the cider made, the whole countryside would come to visit. The dumplings and the cider made it the best night of the year.

Every morning, Sundays included, he left our home in Belfast at half-past five or six to cycle to work at the stables. Sunday was a half day and some weeks he had a free day on Saturday. When I was able to go with him during school holidays, the treat was to share his eggnog before we left.

He beat up two eggs in a bowl, stirred in a little sugar, and added a pint or so of weak tea, strained through a sieve. The egg cooked lightly in the hot tea, like the Chinese way of breaking an egg into soup, and the delicious smell and taste of it is one of the most vivid memories of my youth.

When I was ten or eleven years of age we went for walks together, but always in the city. He was a countryman at heart and had worked there all his life, but he lived in Belfast and had a countryman's love of the city.

For him it was a mixture of awe and fascination. The rows of shops in Sandy Row selling food, shoes, furniture, hardware, drew him every week. He would visit the blacksmith and the saddler just off the Row and would buy cooked pigs' feet to eat when we reached home. After months of persuasion, I tried them. They were delicious.

Further away but visited just as often, was the covered Smithfield Market with its second-hand shops for books and clothes, some piled high with old furniture, stalls selling pets, sheet music, jewellery, jokes and fancy dress. This was his entertainment at the week-end.

His favourite stall was the one which sold army surplus equipment. As World War 2 drew to a close, it became a treasure chest of the finest kit from the British and American forces. He knew the owner and, although he never took me walking or cycling in the country, once he realised my interest in the outdoor life, he would arrive home with something special.

There was a folding Primus Stove with a special clip to attach it to the bar of a bicycle, a US army bivouac tent fastened along the ridge by a double row of buttons, a set of camping dixies, a portable cork-screw, the screw of which fitted into the bamboo handle, a poncho-style cape which could also be a ground-sheet.

For me it was the ideal encouragement. It was better than telling me where to go or even taking me there. It created an excitement for the journey which lasted a lifetime.

One day as we walked down Sandy Row he stopped to talk to a nattily dressed man wearing a yellow cravat and with his hat at a jaunty angle. They seemed to know each other very well. When we left the man and walked on, my father said quietly,

"Just as well I know him, he's the best pick pocket in Ireland."

There was a shout behind us.

"Bert, you've forgotten something." My father was 'Bert' and I was called Bertie' then, a name I disliked. It was the man with the yellow cravat calling after us. From his upstretched hand a watch dangled on its silver chain.

I had never heard him swear but my father was muttering under his breath as he strode back to meet the man half-way.

"It won't do, Bert," said the yellow cravat. "You'll have to be more vigilant. Some rogue of a pick pocket will steal the watch and chain from off your waistcoat."

My father was always smartly dressed on the walks, polished brown boots, narrow trousers, hacking jacket over a fancy waistcoat, collar and tie and a neat racing man's cap, like the very smartest style of Belfast 'duncher'.

Sometimes on a Saturday evening we would walk to the Albert Clock near the centre of town. It was much further but the Custom House Steps were nearby. This was Belfast's Speakers' Corner. His favourite soap-box orator was 'the Atheist'. Heckled by shouts from the crowd quoting Bible texts, the Atheist could match every text with another. The subject would be alcohol and the heckler would roar,

"Wine is a mocker. Strong drink is raging. Proverbs 20, verse 1."

The speaker was quick on the draw, his riposte instantaneous.

"What about 1st Timothy 5, verse 23. Drink no longer water, but use a little wine for thy stomach's sake and thine often infirmities."

My father was no atheist himself but having missed an Ulster Protestant grounding in the Old and New Testaments, his admiration for this particular speaker was boundless.

"He must know every verse in the whole Bible," he would say. "It doesn't matter what they shout, he'll find one to top them."

The Sladers were a yeoman family, he would tell me. I looked up the word in a dictionary but knew that definition was not exactly what he meant. It was only when I went to Devon many years later and stayed with Mary Yelland-Moore, a farmer of yeoman stock herself, that I understood what he had been trying to tell me.

Yeomen were neither gentry nor servants. They were farmers who worked their land themselves, not through the services of an agent. In time of conflict the nobility were powerless without them. But above all, to be a yeoman in Devon was to be your own man.

Even though he worked for the gentry all his life, my father never once gave me the impression that he felt they were of some superior class. And I never knew him to regard anyone as his inferior either. When he spoke to a noble lord or the blacksmith or an unemployed man from the next street he was the same man.

Once I tried to win one of the many friendly arguments we would have, this one about some Irish question, by asking him what he thought he would know about Ireland, him being only an Englishman. His answer showed a rare flash of irritation.

"I'm not an Englishman," he said firmly, "I'm a Devonshire man."

There was no further explanation. Perhaps I failed to ask. It puzzled me for years, in the way that someone from outside Northern Ireland might find it hard to understand why some Ulstermen see no contradiction in believing themselves to be both Irish and British.

When the Romans finally left Britain in the 5th century AD, the invasions of the Angles, the Jutes and the Saxons drove many Celtic families from Devon to Northern France. Six hundred years later, William, Duke of Normandy, gathered an army to invade England, and the Norman Celts were amongst the first to volunteer. When they reached the south-west counties they were rewarded with gifts of land and found the Celtic tongue still the language of the common people.

My son Dion took the family name back to England when he went to work there and he discovered that 'Slader' came from a Norman French word and meant 'the dweller in a forest glade'. His first visit was to Devon to seek out Hunnawins Farm and although his grandfather had left there eighty years before, there were people in the area who seemed to know his family well.

Later we visited Hunnawins together and were given a family tree which took the line back to a Norman family of the 15th century. In the Domesday Book the name appears as Seleda and this was how teachers from England pronounced my name when I first went to grammar school.

The family tree showed that the Slader home in the 15th century was on the other side of the River Bray from Hunnawins, near a village called Charles. In the Domesday book Charles was recorded as Carmes and was the holding of a lay tenant-in-chief, Robert de Pontchardon, a Norman baron.

Although he had never seen the family tree, my father knew that the Sladers had lived near Charles for centuries before his grandfather William came to Hunnawins at the beginning of the 19th century and built a home there. When he was adamant that he was not English, did he mean that his forbears were Norman Celts not Anglo-Saxons?

Six years ago I made a journey, mainly on foot from the north-west of

Spain to the southern coast of Portugal. I walked through the remote hill country of Galicia and crossed the frontier into the mountains of Northern Portugal. After about ten days I reached the ruins of an ancient Celtic village. It was built on a hill with spectacular views over miles of countryside. It was called Citánia de Briteiros, the last Celtic stonghold in Northern Iberia to fall to the Roman invaders in the 1st century BC.

I sat in the ruins of a circular house and felt at home. It was as if some ancient folk memory had been aroused from centuries of slumber, enabling me to sense the spirit of the place. That moment changed the pace of the journey. Until that point the demon of urgency had driven me on. Now I was ready to travel at the journey's own speed. I had touched the past and it made the present accessible with ease and in its full dimensions.

What would my father have made of it? And if he had felt as I did, would he have been able to tell me? When I left the Celtic village I knew, that all those years ago, I had learned much more from him than had been told in words. The spirit of this place had let me hear the echoes of his folk memories.

....

My father's stories of North Devon were of his family and of Exmoor. My grandmother, Sarah, who died the year before I was born, had a horse which no one else could handle. It was a one-eyed black mare so fierce that even my grandfather, who was known as a horseman, left the mare alone. When she drove in her trap to market in North Molton, the road cleared to make way for the black horse and Sarah Slader.

At home I mentioned that we had to read Lorna Doone as part of the English course at school. It was rare for my father to pass any comment about school work but this time I knew he had something important to say. He was a practical man who felt book learning had passed him by but Lorna Doone was different.

It was based on a true story, he explained quietly. I had never known him to read a book or to talk about literature. I tried to tell him that Lorna Doone was a novel and that a novel was a story made up by the author.

With what I see now as great patience, he explained that his mother had told him about Lorna Doone. A man called Blackmore was the author and she had seen the book when it first came out. Mr Blackmore had lived in the village of Charles when he was writing Lorna Doone. She had said too, that the Blackmore family had been connected to the Sladers by marriage many years before.

Her maiden name was Ridd and it was her family who were part of the Lorna Doone story. The Doones were a tribe who had come from Scotland to Exmoor and taken over a sheltered valley as their homestead. It was not the place visited by tourists but another combe in the area. My father knew the name of the combe but it was soon forgotten by me.

I thought of telling my English teacher at school but I was a new boy and decided against.

When Dion and I went to Lynton I found a book in a second-hand shop, probably written in the nineteen thirties by Sir Atholl Oakley. It had as a title 'The Facts On Which Blackmore Based Lorna Doone.' On the front page it said that the book gave 'the official location of the Doone Valley' and Blackmore was quoted as stating that Lorna Doone 'is not a novel'.

My father often spoke of his uncle Richard. My grandfather David and his brother Richard seemed to find it hard to agree. According to my father, David was a hard-working farmer but also a very convivial man. He was a regular at the Poltimore Arms and many an evening it was his horse who found the way back to Hunnawins while David slept the journey through.

Richard never married. Even as a boy he was eccentric, preferring books to farm work. He wrote poetry and Methodist hymns and in his writings always referred to Hunnawins as 'Honey Wins'. He left the farm to set up home by himself in a cottage nearby and earned a living by selling eggs, potatoes, fruit, wild nuts or any portable commodity he could find a market for. As he travelled the countryside of North Devon he became a familiar local character and known as the Pedlar Poet of Exmoor.

Thirty years ago my distant cousin John (our grandfathers were brothers) who lives in Wales, wrote a book about Richard called 'Dicky Slader, the Exmoor Pedlar Poet'. My father died two years before it was published but this was one book he would have read and found fascinating. Most of the tales he told me were in it, though sometimes with a quite different slant.

John's story of the man my father always called Richard was a celebration of Dicky's life and, although now long out of print, is probably the main reason why Dicky is still one of the legendary characters of the West Country.

Richard the Pedlar travelled the country roads and tracks to South Molton, Barnstaple, Porlock, anywhere within walking distance where there was a fair or a market. He carried his wares on his back across the moor to sell to holiday visitors at Lynton on the north coast. His goods might weigh as much as half a hundredweight and eventually be bought a donkey who could carry twice as much and so allow him to expand his trade. On a bad night in winter the donkey would be allowed to sleep in the kitchen of the cottage out of the wind and rain.

John Slader told a story of one of Richard's epic journeys across Exmoor on the way back from selling fresh peas at Lynton. The route is called the Chains and crosses a remote, exposed stretch of the moor. As Richard set out for home that evening the clouds gathered and the wind rose. At the Saddle Gate Stone, where the track ends and the route becomes harder to find across the open moor, a thunder storm swept in from the south-west.

Richard hurried on through the thunder and lightning of the tempest, afraid of being caught out for the night. He reached his cottage as darkness fell. He was soaked and frightened and collapsed in his chair to give thanks to God for his deliverance.

John's story of the walk encouraged Dion and me to follow in Richard's footsteps.

We set out from Lynton early one summer afternoon and the day brightened as we strolled up a wooded valley towards the moor. The route of the Chains was almost due south so we walked towards the sun. The track was good. We climbed to the farm at Shallow Ford sheltering in a little dell, surrounded by rolling pasture, with dozens of horses grazing free on the open land.

The track steepened towards the Saddle Gate Stone. We had walked about five miles and climbed fourteen hundred feet. To the north were spectacular views across the most beautiful Devon countryside, leading down to wooded combes and the coast. Close beside us to the west was a deep, partly wooded valley like an Irish glen.

The track ended at the wind-blown beech trees at the Saddle Gate and we looked for a path to the crest of the moor directly ahead. It was hard to find, the going rough, on tussocks of moor grass and wet bog. In rain and wind this would be hard walking. In mist it would be no easy task to find the way. But we had almost clear skies and a gentle breeze. We reached the crest with shadows across the moor. The spot height on the map was 1566'.

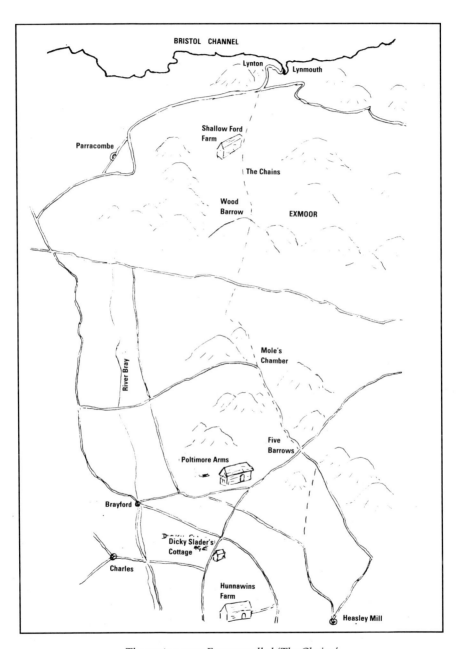

The route across Exmoor called 'The Chains'

The map told us too that this was Wood Barrow, the site of a grave mound, with a small sunken top.

A mile away at the next barrow a party of school children were scattered across the moor like scraps of paper blown on the wind.

It was easy to see why this place had been chosen as an ancient burial site. It was high enough to overlook a huge area of moor and countryside falling away from the ridge on which we stood. The wind was stronger here, we could guess that it was seldom calm in such an exposed position.

Through the thunder and lightning and pouring rain at the height of the storm the Pedlar Poet of Exmoor had passed this way. We were following in his footsteps, but in the very best of travelling weather.

The descent to the road above Challacombe was a pleasant ramble for us but in mist, the grain of the land would make it even more difficult than the ascent on the other side. We walked past Mole's Chamber and followed a country road to Five Barrows.

Here we left Richard's route and walked on to Heasley Mill, where we were staying. It had taken us about five hours from Lynton and we were aware that this would have been only the return journey for Richard. It was almost certain too, that he had left home that morning at dawn on the outward leg.

On his way back Richard would have turned right at Five Barrows and continued to his cottage near Molland Cross without a thought of entering the Poltimore Arms. On such a night as this his brother David was probably inside the inn, warming himself at the fire with a pint pot in his hand.

That evening we ate at the Poltimore Arms. Mary from Heasley Mill had put the word about that we would be there, but we were still surprised to find how many of the locals remembered the family, although Richard, the last to remain in the area, had died sixty years before.

We drank the local cider, the only alcoholic drink of which Richard would have approved. They all called him Dicky as John had done in his book. A local man called Cecil sang us one of Dicky's poems about a straying pig, set to the air 'Should Trelawney Die'.

Before we left Devon, Mary arranged for us to meet an elderly lady called Irene Kelland. She was living in South Molton in the home of Hazel Ansted who was caring for her. Irene looked concerned that we might ask her questions about the family and she might not remember.

Hazel reassured her. Then Dion produced a copy of the family tree and

Irene told him that her grandmother's name was Susannah. Dion pointed to the name on the family tree. Irene's grandmother and my grandfather had been sister and brother.

Irene sat up in the chair, her face radiant, confusion and concern now gone. She was delighted now to be talking to these two strangers from Ireland who had turned out to be relatives.

There was a story she wanted to tell us about Dicky Slader that she had never told before.

When she was a child her parents had lived near Dicky's cottage. Her mother had cared for him by visiting every day and the young Irene would go with her. When Dicky died her mother was sent for. Dicky had left her his few possessions.

When she went to the cottage the only things of any value were six turkey eggs for hatching. Dicky had reared turkeys since he was a boy and his eggs were highly prized. When he was selling them he sometimes said that he had laid them himself.

Irene's mother sold the eggs and bought a gold watch for her daughter with the proceeds. Irene pulled back her sleeve. On her arm was the gold watch bought by Dicky's eggs, still keeping good time.

Dicky would have been pleased to be so remembered. And I felt that he would have been pleased too, by John's book and that his great nephew from Ireland and his great-great nephew had been to the Chains and followed his footsteps across Exmoor.

PILGRIMS' FOOTSTEPS REVISITED

On a Tuesday morning in June nine years ago, I set out on my own to follow the old pilgrim road from France to Santiago de Compostela in Spain. The previous Friday I had left my job with the Sports Council in Northern Ireland, an organisation I had worked for, for twenty-three years. The walk was about 550 miles and I thought it would take me about five weeks to do it.

All my life I had been interested in the outdoors. My first journey began in my early teens, as a walk from my home in West Belfast to the summit of one of the hills of South Antrim which overlooked the city. The view across the mountains, lakes and coast of Ulster led to a four-day cycle trip around the Province with an even younger friend. The adventure inspired a lifetime of journeys and when I wrote about it many years later, I called it, *'Beyond the Black Mountain'*.

My travels took me to Europe and Asia and to climb in the Alps, the Pyrenees and Arctic Norway. In the seventies I led mountaineering expeditions to Iran and Afghanistan and in the eighties I trekked with two friends across the Himalayas to the borders of Tibet.

Now, having left full-time employment, it was time for another journey, this time on my own.

In 1985 there was very little up-to-date information available on the pilgrimage to Santiago. I could find no guide book or map, only a leaflet from Spanish Tourism outlining the route for those travelling by car.

Then I discovered that Walter Starkie, Irish academic, writer and diplomat, had written a book in the forties called *'The Road to Santiago'*. I bought the large scale maps for Northern Spain, ringed all the towns and villages mentioned by Starkie and began my own journey.

I started at St. Jean Pied-de-Port in France and set off on the first stage across the Pyrenees with perhaps greater excitement and hopes than on any previous venture. I was aware that this was more of a step into the unknown than any previous journey, not just in the physical sense that the land and the people would be new to me, but that it would be an entirely different experience.

After four days I reached Puente la Reina in Spain, a little town which had grown up around a beautiful bridge across the Rio Agra. It had been built for pilgrims in the 11th century, with six elegant arches of golden stone and still in use 900 years later. Puente was the place where the four great medieval pilgrim routes from Northern Europe met to form one road, the Camino de Santiago.

Although I was not aware of it at the time, at Puente la Reina my journey changed from long-distance walk to pilgrimage.

During the first few days I had felt a loneliness which quenched the appetite and kept me travelling on with hardly a pause. For someone used to travelling on his own it was a surprise, a salutary shock to the system of one so self-sufficient, so independent. It was only months later that, having heard the story, a voice from the crowd said.

"You had so much to share but no one to share it with."

At the inn in Puente I met my first pilgrim. He was a German, some years older than myself, who had made a vow at the abbey in Vézelay in France to follow the road of St. James. He had been walking for thirty days and was footsore and weary. From him I learned about the modern pilgrimage to Santiago, about cheap accommodation along the way, places to see, pilgrim lore, stories of the Camino.

Some days later he told me he had been tempted that evening to give up and return home but I had cheered him on his way. Bruno was a sincere, devout man and through him I began to understand the Cult of St. James.

He called me a peregrino, a pilgrim, and when he realised that it was more than I felt could be claimed for someone on my journey, he said,

"You and I travel to Santiago for different reasons, but we are on the same road."

Bruno and I never walked together, but for a time we met every few evenings at an inn. For me he was the real pilgrim. The further I walked towards Santiago the more I sensed the mystical power of the Camino and found it easier to accept Bruno's view that I too, was a peregrino.

The journey changed my life and I knew I would come back. And four years later I set out along the Road to Santiago again.

Once again I started in France but this time I joined the ancient road that came from Arles. It was used in medieval times by hundreds of thousands of pilgrims from Italy and Provence. This was the most southerly route of the four specified in the 12th century Pilgrim's Guide, the Codex Calixtinus.

The other three routes started further north, in Paris, Vézelay and Le Puy and met near St Jean Pied-de-Port where I began my first walk. They were joined in Spain at Puente la Reina by the route from Arles and from there the Codex stated that 'a single road leads to St. James'.

Oloron Ste Marie is about sixty kilometres north of the Pyrenees near Pau and Lourdes. I made the bridge there my starting point on a sunny afternoon in July. A main road climbs south towards the Col du Somport, one of the principal passes over the Pyrenees, but there was a quiet country road on the other side of the river which was pleasant walking. Once again I stepped out on the Road to Santiago in hope and with great expectations.

At Lurbe-St.-Christau everywhere seemed closed and shuttered except the inn. It was not a small village but there was neither shop nor café. Most of the houses had 'For Sale' notices. I saw no one in the shady streets. There was a room free in the small hotel and my notes remind me of my stay. 'Good room with a pleasant view. Fair meal. Poor wine.' It was a melancholy start.

At the beginning of my previous journey the days had been lonely and I had been the only one staying at the inns. The food and the wine however, had cheered the evenings.

For another day and a half I climbed towards the pass and let the little roads and lanes take me closer to the mountains. I passed an old hotel, now closed, with the letters 'H S J' carved high on the wall. Once it was the Hotel St. Jacques, now it seemed to be a private residence, faded grandeur at the front, Satellite TV dish and pelotta court at the back.

Bedous was a fine ancient village but all the shops were closed and the houses shuttered. Borce was another picturesque old hamlet but here too the streets were empty and there was neither shop nor café. Had this part of France closed down for the summer?

I asked a man near the church if there was a shop or a bar. He shrugged a monumental Gallic shrug.

"There is nothing here," he said, "The rich come from the cities and buy all the houses. They rarely stay here and when they do, their food and wine come with them." He pointed at the boot of an expensive car parked in a narrow space beside one of the dwellings.

The valley narrowed and tunnelled into the cliffs on the east side was a fortress, its gun emplacements and observation galleries still menacing above. I had been this way before by car, but for the first time I sensed its past. The villages and the fortress might look dead but the pass still lived and

I was travelling at a pace which let me feel it.

I left the road and followed a track through scrub land and forest to the Col du Somport. Even in the mist it was a place of scenic grandeur. I glimpsed the peaks and the valley dropping steeply down to France. On the great stones which marked the frontier there was carved the sword of St. James.

Only one hotel in the ski resort of Cadanchu was open and I took a room. My notes said, 'Monstrous on the outside, tasteful inside, South American nose-flute music from 6:30 a.m. to 11:30 p.m.'

Nearby great machines were ripping the mountainside apart to build more hotels and apartment blocks. A bizarre picture flashed in my mind of this place full of life and frantically busy in the ski season, and dead and deserted the rest of the year.

At Canfranc a young man asked me if I was 'the elderly Dutchman' he was waiting for. He was wrong on all three counts! And, dear reader, before you smile and pity me, I should say he was about nineteen years of age and probably thought of everyone over thirty-five as 'elderly'.

My spirits soared when I found the first of the yellow arrows which point the way to Santiago. It took me off the surfaced road and as I followed it down, a shepherd passed with a huge flock of sheep heading up to summer pastures. It was the way his forebears and their flocks would have used for centuries.

I crossed the river by an ancient hump-backed bridge near a ruined church. Once the little church had a very steeply pitched roof. The snow falls must be heavy here. Its upper windows were still impressive.

In a simple hotel at Villanua, a framed notice told me that King Carlos and Queen Sofia had lunched here on the way up to the skiing. Although they had stayed at the Hotel Edelweiss at Cadanchu, they had come back here to dine. I was not in the least surprised.

The notice told me that the royal couple had ordered cabrito a la horna (roast young goat) and if it was as good as the conejo con ali-oli (rabbit with a garlic sauce) which I had, they had made the right choice. The wine of Aragon was good too, and I stayed the night in some comfort.

The yellow arrows were sporadic, elusive. A few would appear and draw me on, then there would be none for miles. I wandered down through lanes overgrown with thorny bushes and, at the end of the afternoon, stepped off a track on to one of the main streets of Jaca.

When I came here first in the sixties, Jaca was an intriguing frontier town with an army base in an ancient fortified encampment. The presence of soldiers might have dominated the town but for the university with its famous cultural summer school and a market which drew farmers from a huge area of the surrounding countryside. To cross the Pyrenees and come here was to step back fifty years in time, to a Spain before the Civil War.

Now it was transformed, new buildings, elegant shops, massive apartment blocks, cafés, discos, all in Euro-ski style. Although south of the mountains, the town is close enough to the snow slopes to attract huge numbers of skiers in season. Their money will pay for Jaca's new affluence.

I searched for the old town and found it more elusive than the yellow arrows. Where once I had eaten well in Spanish style, there was an expensive ski-tourist menu and no local wines. Only the cathedral still seemed to stand firm against the invasion.

Then I found a pleasant place to stay in the old part of the town. Beside it was a bar where I had an excellent fish soup, lamb chops grilled on an open fire and the local rosado wine. Jaca and I were friends again.

For days I travelled almost due west. There should have been a wonderful stretch of the Camino above the Rio Aragon but there was no yellow arrow. I asked a local man and he shook his head as if disappointed for me. It was now all 'campo' he told me, one huge ploughed field. The old route had gone.

I walked the shore of the reservoir on the Rio Aragon called Mar del Pirineo, the Pyrenean Sea, and climbed a hill to the deserted village of Tiermas. The villagers had been moved when their land was submerged under the waters of the dam. Now the houses were slowly crumbling away. Part of the roof of the church had caved in. Once the pilgrims would have climbed up the steep hill and walked this cobbled street at the end of another day's hard travelling

Nearby was the Monastario de Leyre and the church at Sanguesa where on my first visit here twenty-five years before, I had been intrigued by the stone carvings.

At the time I had no knowledge of the Santiago pilgrimage, nor of its traditional routes. When I reached Puente la Reina on my first journey on the Camino, Bruno had told me I must visit the church there before I left in the morning. On the door pillars were carved figures in the same style as those I had photographed all those years before at Leyre and Sanguesa.

The heat was rising in the mornings, so an early start was essential. There was welcome shade in a spectacular gorge called the Foz de Lumbier, the old route following the river deep in a cleft between the rocks. Where the path should have crossed the Rio Irati, the ancient bridge was down, but a tunnel led to a new bridge to the north.

At lunch time I rested on a flat rock beside the river. There were deep pools and shade from bushes growing out of cracks in the rock. A cliff opposite caught the sun and it was alive with swifts darting to and from high perches. It was the most serene moment of the walk.

I stayed the night at a road-side inn and soaked the afternoon heat away in the early evening, in the luxury of its outdoor pool. My room was a cool haven after the scorching heat. Here, the evening meal at 9:30 p.m. makes sense. I had fish soup again. Bruno had once told me in his serious, always helpful way that the peregrino must have soup each evening. He was right of course, but not only in theory, the body yearned for it, in taste and substance.

I had grilled merluza (hake) with a tomato salad and tried the rosado of Aragon again just to be sure I liked it. At the end of the meal, the owner of the hostal came over to sit with me. He brought me a liqueur of the Pyrenees, slightly sweet, aromatic with mountain herbs, the perfect way to end the meal.

The next day was meant to be the last day and I started out in good spirits after such a pleasant overnight. But the route was partly surfaced road and the day became hot early. It was not an exceptionally long walk in kilometres, but the dusty road and the heat made it as hard travelling as ever I had faced.

I reached the solitary church of Eunate, built in the 12th century, set on its own in brown landscape below a rocky ridge, baking in the mid-summer heat. The church is octagonal, ringed by a colonnade within a wall which separates church ground from campo. It was worth every kilometre of the arduous day's grind.

As if by prior arrangement, the caretaker arrived to open the church and I was able to sit and rest in the cool interior. It was tiny inside. If, as I had been told, it was modelled on the Holy Sepulchre in Jerusalem, then it was in miniature and atmospheric, intimate because of that.

The map showed that I had five kilometres to go and I set off to follow the direction of the yellow arrow on a nearby wall. An hour should do it.

Half an hour's steady climbing later I reached the ridge and could see immediately that it was the wrong direction. A false trail when the legs are fresh or on an easy day is not difficult to bear but towards the end of a long, exhausting day in the heat it wrings out the spirits through a mangle.

The yellow arrows had been evident only intermittently during the whole trip, but they had always been welcome when they did appear. Now I intended to follow the map. I walked on through the hottest time of the day to the point where the four great medieval roads to Santiago finally become one. It is marked by a black metal statue of a pilgrim in medieval dress, with scallop shell on his hat, pilgrim staff, script and gourd.

I walked down into Puente la Reina, through its narrow main street, straight to the pilgrim bridge of golden stone. I had been here before. It was in Puente la Reina that my first journey on the Camino de Santiago had changed its character. Here Bruno had called me a peregrino.

Puente la Reina had changed, I thought at first, but only superficially. It was a holiday week-end and the crowds from Pamplona were here for the day. The old Puente soon re-established itself however, timeless, serene, unmoved by this flash of popularity.

Beside the bridge a man came out of an archway which seemed to be the only entrance to a house. He was dressed for the fields and behind him, from the same archway, emerged a herd of about a dozen cows. They were being driven from behind by a teenage girl with a stout stick. In County Antrim it would be called a bullock walloper, and she was using it persuasively, firmly.

An older woman followed, brushing up the straw and dung. This was the main street of the town and she was determined that it would be clean outside her front door.

I was not to know that I would be back here again less than two years later. This time I would not be alone, but accompanied by sixty-four companions, all set to step out on the Camino, ready for the great journey to Santiago.

The new venture began almost as soon as I reached home after this walk. Lorna from MS Ireland, the Multiple Sclerosis charity, rang me at home. Someone had found a copy of *'Pilgrims' Footsteps'* at RTE, she told me, and had suggested that the Road to Santiago should be their next sponsored walk. She wanted to know if she and the walk leader could come to see me in Newcastle to help them plan the route.

Lorna and Donncha, the organiser and the leader of the walk, came to County Down. They told me they hoped to have over sixty walkers, each of whom would have to raise almost £2,000 in sponsorship for the charity to be eligible to go. We planned a ten day route. Donncha recorded an interview with me about my own walk to Santiago for his popular radio programme on RTE, Donncha's Sunday. I wished them well.

The walk was a wonderful success. The sixty-odd walkers raised a huge sum for the support of people with MS and their families. MS Ireland gained a new group of friends and allies. Public awareness of MS was greatly increased through the press and radio coverage of the walk.

I had another telephone call from Lorna later the same year. This time she was not asking for advice. We met on neutral ground, in Dundalk.

"They're a grand crowd," she said persuasively. "Super people. Great crack." She wanted me to lead the walk the following year.

I offered advice and encouragement. I bobbed and weaved like a boxer trying to stay out of trouble. It was no use. She was not listening.

It was time to come clean. It meant telling her that having led groups for years at home and abroad, I had decided that I had done my bit. All that was yesterday and a little voice had whispered in my ear "Never again". It was someone else's turn.

Lorna was still not listening. Patiently she told me of the huge effort the walkers make to raise funds for MS and of the work of MS Ireland. Anything I might be able to do as leader seemed very small in comparison.

She neglected to tell me about the aggravations. The fast crowd who were afraid to pause to look at the day in case their feet took root. The mimics who thought the Ulster accent was their special gift from St. James himself. The experts on every topic, Spanish or Irish, sport or wine, food or photography.

We started at the end of May, at the statue of the pilgrim just outside Puente la Reina. There were sixty-four of us from Ireland, North and South. From Tyrone and Donegal, Wexford and Waterford. Cork and West Cork, Kerry, Mayo, Meath, Antrim and Down. In fact from every corner of the island.

We had two hundred miles or so in front of us, on ten one-day stages of the Camino. I stood to one side and looked them over. They were wearing MS tee-shirts and shorts, with trainers or boots. They scampered about taking photographs, smiling at me trustingly, keenness personified, talking so excitedly I could hardly hear myself think.

It was a cool day, with the prospect of rain. I appointed two of the group to act as walk leaders for the day, to find the way and set the pace. I had asked two others to act as sweepers at the back and two to help me within the group. There were a number of experienced walkers in the party, so I would have no shortage of volunteers, but I had it in mind to involve everyone during the course of the ten days.

Noreen stepped up to the statue and said a prayer for a safe journey. She asked for a blessing for those who would benefit from the funds raised, for our families and friends, for us on the walk. It was a moving moment, even for those who did not believe.

We were on our way, laughing and talking, cheerfully, nervously. These were the first steps. There was a long way to go.

We passed through Puente la Reina and walked across the bridge. The yellow arrows led us along the river, past olive groves and vineyards where the vines had been pruned hard, stumps only a foot high, buds not as developed as those on my vine before I left home. The birds sang from amongst the trees along the river. We rose through scrub land and parched hills to cross a ridge and a road.

There were a few small hamlets but little habitation in between. In one village the route took us through the porch of the church and down a magnificent stretch of Roman road to an almost collapsed Roman bridge. We crossed on the single arch still left, precariously, by a narrow crumbling ledge.

From near the back I could hear roars of laughter further up the line. I heard the details later. Jimmy the actor-manager and Bob the honky-tonk piano player were swopping stories about a character called Duffy who had once worked for Guinness in Dublin.

Jimmy started, even Bob could never get the word in first. When His Holiness, the Pope, came to Ireland Duffy wanted to impress a Protestant workmate. "There's one thing about our Pope your Protestant ministers don't have." Duffy knew he was on firm ground on this one. " Our Pope is inflammable."

Duffy worked in a shed in the yard and one damp day a mate came in to see him. "Jasus Duff," he says, "That glass is terrible. It's very hot in here." "That's not the heat," says Duffy, "That's the condescension."

Eventually Bob got one in. Apparently Duffy's bowels were reluctant to move. "Me mother says." said Duffy confidentially, "I'm emancipated."

Six hours later we reached the beautiful town of Estella in the sunshine, a most important resting place on the Camino since medieval times. One day down and nine to go. Everyone seemed to have managed the stage well, a few blisters, some tight muscles. It augured well for the rest of the walk.

Day Two took us through the Rioja wine region. Gravelled tracks scrunched underfoot. The cool morning became hot and the tracks dusty. Lorna had arranged a visit to a Bodega at lunchtime. The tour of the winery was long and thorough but the rewards were delicious tapas snacks and fine wine.

In the afternoon we climbed through the heat to the crest of a ridge and Dan roared an encouragement from Cork. We crossed the plains to Santo Domingo and a band played as we entered the town, as if to welcome us. In the cathedral there is a magnificent wooden chicken coop, ornately carved, high on one wall, and in it a live cock and a hen to commemorate a miracle of the Pilgrimage.

Day Three took us to the tiny, remote village of San Juan de Ortega beyond the mountains of Oca. The village had only eight inhabitants but there was a large Romanesque church. The priest invited us inside for a blessing. It was cool, almost cold after the heat of the track. His voice echoed as he spoke quickly in Spanish. I asked Mary to translate.

He says he has received ten thousand pilgrims here, Mary told me. That this is a place for everyone, for all the world. Remarkable things have happened here. People leave this village set against the material world, feeling that they can set the world free. But the most important thing is to be a pilgrim. And don't deny it. Being pilgrims will change us. And we must change ourselves. It is the only way to change the world.

It was important that those who wanted to pray, found time to do so in their own way on the Camino. Relaxation was important too, prayer in its own fashion.

That evening after dinner Irene stilled the chatter with a haunting Irish song, in a quiet, pure tone which would have filled a cathedral.

It was essential that we finished to-day without being too exhausted. The next stage was a long one across the great tableland of the Meseta.

We started from a small village near Burgos. On my own journey I had begun the stage in the city itself, ten kilometres further back and knew we had a tough day in front of us. But I knew too, it would be a magnificent walk across the Meseta, an almost empty, sun-burnt landscape with small villages, spaced miles apart, tucked into deep valleys, cut into the table land by the rivers.

I remembered this vast undulating plateau with its fields of poppies, shaking and swaying in the sunshine, and sitting down to watch the poppies dance.

As we climbed the track now, it became the hottest day so far, the track hard baked clay, the feet scuffling in its dust. In the late afternoon we passed under the arch of the ruined Hospital de San Anton, where pilgrims were cared for 800 years before.

There was every sign that the tiredness of the whole journey, was making this the hardest day. We saw the village of Castrojeriz built around the side of a prominent hill, but I had to warn our party that this is a long village, that we had still a mile to walk once we reached its outskirts.

There were sighs of relief when the stage was finished. There was the ecstatic joy of sitting down with no further to walk, litres of cool liquids to be drunk, dozens of blisters for the attention of Niamh, our physiotherapist, fast becoming Ireland's foremost blister expert.

That night the entertainment at dinner was not merely a diversion. The spirits needed a mighty lift. We had six more days to go. Marie led with delightful operetta. Jim sang some of his songs which became our songs of the Camino. Tom, the show band man, gave us a sad air from Mayo. Frank and Pakie, the mimics, did funny walks of pilgrim walkers, imitations of any of us brave enough to open our mouths in front of them earlier that day and a victory speech from General Norman Schwarzkopt who some seemed to confuse with Dermod. Then Carmel, the Entertainer, entertained us. This crew would be ready to face the next day, of that there was no doubt whatsoever.

Day Five was memorable because of the village in which we finished. It was down-at-heel, nondescript in appearance but the welcome appeared on the faces of the villagers. We sat in the sunshine in a narrow street and entertained ourselves. Then they joined us and before we left, sang us some of the old songs of the Camino.

The next two days would remain in the memories of all of us as long as we lived.

On day six we climbed high into the mountains of Berzio to the deserted village of Foncebadon where I had met the wild dogs. The pack was friendly now, no doubt placated by tit-bits from peregrinos.

We stopped at the iron cross perched high on a great mound of stones carried here by pilgrims over the centuries. We threw our own stones with a prayer or a blessing, for those for whom we were walking, for everyone at home.

It was a quiet, emotive time, reminding us why we were here. Even those who did not know it at the time, were changed by our little ceremony. The group had changed, as if we understood the true nature of our purpose. Maybe we all knew now what it was like to be a pilgrim, whether or not we were prepared to acknowledge the Pilgrimage of St. James.

A track, once the line of a Roman road led through grassy meadows, then on a rough, rocky path down the steep side of a gorge. This was my kind of country, the walking which suited me best, but for some of the party, the heat and the stony path made it their hardest physical challenge so far.

Hours later, at the foot of the gorge, and to the cheers and applause of those who had arrived before us, we crossed a Roman bridge into the village of Molinaseca. The hostal which welcomed us was on the river-side below the bridge. It was an idyllic end to a stage, if ever there was one.

Although everyone looked tired, there was a communion of spirit, a sense of joy, a strength of purpose which I knew would carry us on to the very end of this journey, and well beyond it. We would never forget this day, nor, I thought, would any of us ever regret it.

Day Seven meant another ascent, this time much steeper. I divided the party into three groups, each with a leader and sweepers and, for once, walked on my own. We climbed an ancient track through villages far from main roads. High in spectacular mountain terrain we crossed into the Province of Galicia.

John and Pat and others from the first group came back to join me, to see if anyone in the last group needed help. But the last party needed no such assistance. They climbed the track towards us singing, and singing we walked into O Cebrero, the place I had called 'the village in the clouds'

The soup at the Hostal San Giraldo would have pleased Bruno. It was a meal in itself. The little church was built in the 12th century and contains relics in a famous chalice which commemorate another of the miracles of the Camino.

Days Eight and Nine led us through the beautiful Galician countryside, wooded with oaks and eucalyptus trees and there were tiny villages connected by tracks I had called 'the lanes of enchantment'. At times the way seemed long, further than when I had been on my own.

We came down into the valley of the Rio Miño at a point where a dam had meant the moving of a village to a site on the far hillside. Portomarin has a fortress church originally built by the Knights of St. John. It was moved, stone by numbered stone, to the new site, its great rose window still above a Romanesque square.

By popular demand Frank set himself up as my interpreter that evening at dinner. Apparently when I told them 'It's only another five kilometres', it meant there was still a two-hour walk to do. When I said I thought it might be a 'warmish day', they knew I meant hotter than hot, 'a wee hill', was a huge mountain, 'an odd skiffle of rain' was a downpour.

The heat had been increasing over the past few days, but on the morning of the last day it started hotter than ever. The temperatures reached the nineties and that day Galicia was the hottest part of Europe. At one point we struggled along the main road in single file, heat baking down from above, reflecting up from the road at our feet. One of the hardiest of all the walkers came over when we paused for a short break.

"I don't mind telling you, Bert," he said wearily, "When we stopped here, the legs just went from under me."

We lunched in the shade beside a chapel at Monte del Gozo, overlooking Santiago. In the afternoon we tramped down into the pilgrim city and through its labyrinthine streets. They insisted that I led this last stretch and for the first time on the walk I led from the front.

Bells rang in the distance. From closer to, Galician flute music danced lightly in the air. We passed under the shade of an archway and emerged into the sunlight in the huge square, the Plaza del Obradorio, in front of the cathedral.

I felt as if a great sigh of relief swept from my body. We had done it. We had all made it safely. Lorna was there to meet us. There were shouts of joy, cries of congratulation and tears, the sweet tears of happiness. There were hugs and handshakes. For ten days and over two hundred miles we had walked together and found a kind of friendship which might elude others for a lifetime. We had arrived in Santiago.

I had invited Jim and Gerry to lead us into the cathedral but they all insisted that Lorna and I go to the top of the steps to receive them before the Portal of Glory. Like hundreds of thousands of pilgrims before us, we entered the cathedral and gave thanks for a safe journey. It was time to celebrate.

When I arrived here on my own it had been quite different. There was no great surge of joy. It had been a solitary experience. I sat in the calm of the dim interior of the cathedral and let my self feel the tiredness of the day and the deeper fatigue of the whole journey. The tension of modern life had gone. There was a feeling of calmness and relaxation, a sense of peace. I was aware then that it would be a new beginning for me, not an end.

The next two years saw two more walks to Santiago organised by MS Ireland. Some of the stages were changed. My own special treat was that we now chose to start the first stage in France near St. Jean Pied-de-Port and thus began by crossing the Pyrenees. We all reached Santiago and received our pilgrim certificates, the famous Compostelas.

A journey back through time
To feel the raod as they did

Many of those who had been before came again, and again. Some were themselves MS sufferers but happily in remission. There were some who had survived serious illness. Another had defied great odds against survival and lived to walk and cheer us on the way. They were all making this journey for others.

It was having such companions which made the walks for me, each party with a unique character of its own. Sometimes the weather was a little damp, they would say it poured with rain. Some days it was warm, they would say it was baking hot. At times the going might be yielding, they would say it was a bog. But as we walked the Camino together, these people became my friends.

On all the journeys I knew that my companions and I had seen flashes of the real nature of each other. I was proud to have been with every one of them. Like some of the very best things in life it had not been gained without a struggle, but we had been up to it. The whole walk and its final moment when we entered the great square would remain with us. No one would ever be able to take them from us.

Lorna and I are going back to the Camino next week, with over forty companions. If I'm lucky I'll hear Dick's 'Walking the Camino Blues' and Jim sing 'The Dutchman' and see Frank do the Gerry Ryan walk.

We'll share too, one of the great mystical journeys of the world with new friends we'll never forget and walk for a cause which would have the approval of that priest at San Juan de Ortega who knew how to change the world.

Also by the same author

AVAILABLE POST FREE FROM

QUEST BOOKS (NI)

2 Slievenabrock Avenue, Newcastle, Co. Down.
N. Ireland. BT33 0HZ
Telephone: 03967 23359

Footsteps in the Hindu Kush. 100pp. Illustrated. £5.95 (post free)
Tales of the people and the mountains of Afghanistan.

Pilgrims' Footsteps. 184pp. Illustrated. £6.50 (post free)
A walk along the ancient Pilgrim Road to Santiago de Compostela.

Pilgrims' Footsteps. TAPE. 90 minutes audio tape £5.00 (post free)
Stories from the book narrated by the author.

Beyond the Black Mountain. 112pp. Illustrated. £4.95 (post free)
A journey around the Ulster of yesterday. Illustrated by Wilfrid Capper.

Across the Rivers of Portugal. 120 pp. Illustrated. £6.50 (post free)
A journey on foot from Northern Spain to Southern Portugal.